The American Identity
Parts I–IV
Patrick N. Allitt, Ph.D.

PUBLISHED BY:

THE TEACHING COMPANY
4840 Westfields Boulevard, Suite 500
Chantilly, Virginia 20151-2299
1-800-TEACH-12
Fax—703-378-3819
www.teach12.com

Patrick N. Allitt, Ph.D.

Professor of History, Emory University

Patrick N. Allitt is Professor of History at Emory University and Director of Emory's Center for Teaching and Curriculum. He was born and raised in central England and attended schools near his home in Mickleover, Derbyshire. An undergraduate at Hertford College, Oxford, he graduated with honors in British and European History (1977). After a year of travel, he studied for the History doctorate at the University of California, Berkeley (Ph.D., 1986). A postdoctoral fellow at Harvard Divinity School (1985–1988), Professor Allitt then joined the faculty of Emory, where he has worked since the fall of 1998, except for a second postdoctoral fellowship (1992–1993) at Princeton University's Center for the Study of American Religion.

Professor Allitt is the author of four Teaching Company series and five books: *Catholic Intellectuals and Conservative Politics in America, 1950 1985* (1993), *Catholic Converts: British and American Intellectuals Turn to Rome* (1997), *Major Problems in American Religious History* (2000), *Religion in America Since 1945* (2003), and *I'm the Teacher, You're the Student* (2004). His wife, Toni, is American, a Michigan native, and their daughter, Frances, was born in 1988.

Table of Contents
The American Identity

Table of Contents
The American Identity

Table of Contents
The American Identity

The American Identity

Scope:

From the time of the Revolution to the present, Americans have always been self-conscious, aware that their nation represents something unique in the history of the world. A wide variety of American interpreters have explained the nature of this uniqueness, and a wide variety of foreign visitors have joined in, offering interpretations that depend on the contrast between their own countries and what they found on this side of the Atlantic. None of these interpreters has had a more lasting effect, here and abroad, than Alexis de Tocqueville, whose *Democracy in America* appeared before the Civil War but remains an influential explanation of American character and identity. To Tocqueville, America's commitment to human equality and to a democratic political system were the nation's most distinctive attributes.

From the vantage point of the 21st century, this course examines the lives of distinctive Americans as it seeks to answer the question of what makes America special and different. It shows that certain character traits and attitudes, vivid in some of the nation's most creative individuals, have stamped themselves on American life. Among them are, undoubtedly, faith in human equality and faith in political democracy. Other traits include an anti-fatalist outlook, a belief that material and moral progress are possible, high faith in the benefits of education, eagerness to live up to national ideals, intense religiosity, and a belief that individual economic exertion will generate wealth and material development.

Stereotypes can be insulting and can lead us to overlook important variations, but they grow out of real situations and, as a point of contact with social realities, can also be useful guides. The generalizations made in this course about Americans are not to be taken as definitive, nor prescriptive—only descriptive. Inevitably, the character of American identity has gone through profound changes in the two centuries since the Revolution. In the late 18th century, the new United States was overwhelmingly a rural country, most of whose people made their living from farming. Today, it is overwhelmingly urban, with only about three percent of its people still drawing their living directly from the soil. This immense change has been accompanied by others equally great: the annihilation of slavery in a bitter civil war; the transformation in the social roles played by, and expected of, men and women; and the rise of the

United States from provincial obscurity to the status of a world-dominating superpower.

The individuals studied in this course can each be labeled according to how they helped shape the national identity. All can be grouped, first of all, as either idealists or pragmatists (a few clearly put pragmatism at the service of their idealism). Further, the pragmatists can be divided, as an accompanying illustration shows, into several sub-groups: explorers, inventors, entrepreneurs, soldiers, and politicians. The idealists in their turn are subdivided into intellectuals, religious figures, artists, and humanitarians. In addition to these broad categories, each is associated, in the lecture dedicated to his or her work, with a more specific trait. Thus, the lecture on Frederick Douglass is subtitled "The Abolitionist," and the lecture investigates not only his own antislavery work but the wider development of the abolitionist movement in antebellum America, with all its stresses and internal divisions. Similarly, the lecture on Andrew Carnegie is subtitled "Conscience-Stricken Entrepreneur" and describes not only Carnegie's own attempt to distribute the millions he acquired as an iron and steel magnate, but also the frequency with which America's super-rich have become benefactors of education and philanthropy.

The four parts of the course follow a roughly chronological pattern. The first part introduces a series of powerful figures from colonial America, many of whom would have regarded themselves as Englishmen rather than Americans but who nevertheless imparted some of their characteristic imaginativeness, forcefulness, and energy to the American tradition. Among them are the explorer and colonial founder John Smith; the religious liberty advocate, Quaker, and colonial founder William Penn; the great Puritan intellectual Cotton Mather; and the astonishing 18th-century polymath Benjamin Franklin. Part I climaxes with the revolutionary generation and the men and women who had to make the difficult transition from being British subjects to being American citizens. Some among them, such as First Lady Abigail Adams, set the tone and style for a long line of successors.

The second part of the course considers influential Americans of the early 19th century, many of whom knew one another, many of whom were involved in the great controversy over whether the nation would maintain or overthrow the slave system, and who collectively energized the young republic's astonishing economic growth. Two writers from this group,

Ralph Waldo Emerson and Louisa May Alcott, bear witness to the maturing of a distinctive American literary and philosophical culture.

Part III, picking up the story after the convulsions of the Civil War, highlights the men and women who turned America into a first-class industrial nation dedicated to sustained economic growth and who enabled the republic to stretch, in reality rather than just aspiration, from ocean to ocean. Part IV, finally, bears witness to the nation's development of a global reach in the mid-20th century, personified in such international heroes as the aviator Charles Lindbergh, such war leaders as General Douglas MacArthur, and such international cultural stars as Leonard Bernstein.

A theme of the Teaching Company's seven-part *American History* course is that the nation can be judged harshly if the historian stresses its inability to live up to its high ideals, but that it can be judged more benignly if the historian stresses its actual achievements side by side with the actual achievements of the other developed Western nations. This course offers detailed illustrations of that point, but it also digresses to introduce some figures whose names rarely figure prominently in lists of American heroes and who have been eclipsed by later celebrities. For example, one lecture is devoted to David Rittenhouse and William Bartram, respectively the leading astronomer and naturalist of the late colonial period, who in their day, were honored and preeminent citizens. Another is devoted to Edmund Ruffin, whose paradoxical life reminds us of the need to study historical figures in context. In one respect an apostle of modernity, Ruffin was an early champion of systematic chemical study of soils to detect the nature of fertility decline and to seek ways of repairing it. In another way, he seems an atavistic figure—a dedicated champion of slavery so horrified by its ending after the Civil War that he committed suicide.

Among these lectures, a wide variety of activities is surveyed, each with equal seriousness. The only two figures in this course who became presidents—Thomas Jefferson and Herbert Hoover—are here considered as an intellectual and as a humanitarian, respectively, rather than for their expressly political accomplishments. Musicians, such as Duke Ellington and Leonard Bernstein; the art collector Isabella Stewart-Gardner; and the movie star Shirley Temple get equal time with such conventional figures from the national pantheon as Lewis and Clark and Ralph Waldo Emerson. Historians and educators today rightly emphasize the diversity of the nation's people and heritage. This course tries to honor this diversity by including men and women, Native Americans, African-Americans, Latinos, whites, and a wide variety of immigrants, who brought childhood experiences from abroad to their new American home. The course even includes people from apparently obscure walks of life (which nevertheless had a special importance), such as the Los Angeles water engineer William Mulholland. Collectively, the approximately 50 people studied in this course, though by no means definitive in illuminating the American identity, will nevertheless be highly illustrative of its richness and diversity.

Lecture One
Being American

Scope: This course is a study of the American character, told in the form of a series of biographies of fascinating Americans. Some of them are among the most famous people in the nation's history, including Benjamin Franklin and Thomas Jefferson. Others are more obscure, and you may never have heard of some of them, for example, Edmund Ruffin or William Mulholland. Some are regionally famous, such as Francis Marion of South Carolina, and some are famous to particular religious or ethnic groups, such as the Jewish writer Abraham Cahan. Each one is associated here with a particular activity, and the lectures are subtitled with these activities—for example, "Frederick Douglass—The Abolitionist" or "Samuel Gompers—The Trade Unionist." This course is less focused on following each man or woman from cradle to grave than in showing how he or she is a representative figure for an American activity or characteristic. For example, every detail of Eli Whitney's life will not be followed, but the lecture will try to show how Whitney can be thought of as a representative inventor and how he fits into the wider history of American inventors and inventions.

Outline

I. The meaning of American identity has been controversial for two centuries.

    A. In the 19th century, Alexis de Tocqueville, who probably wrote the most famous study of the American identity, regarded the commitment to human equality as the bedrock of American virtues.

    B. The idea of national character, much disputed among historians, was popular in the early and mid-20th century.

        1. David Potter argued that the American character was defined by the fact of material abundance.

        2. Daniel Boorstin emphasized Americans' inventiveness, adaptability, and pragmatism.

3. Perry Miller wrote books about the "New England mind" or the "American mind," implying that such things could be defined.

C. The social history revolution of the post-1970 era cast doubt on the idea of a national character.

1. Social historians studied the lives and work of particular ethnic groups, emphasizing differences rather than similarities.

2. They pointed out that the idea of certain characteristics being distinctively "American" could even be coercive, as in the politics of the 1950s, when the existence of a Congressional committee—the House Un-American Activities Committee— implied that certain activities and ideas were un-American.

II. Nevertheless, the idea of national character, if defined broadly and carefully, can be useful.

A. Certain characteristics and attitudes do appear, especially to outsiders, as distinctly American, including a lack of fatalism, an energetic approach to problem-solving, faith in human equality and democracy, belief in the boundless possibilities of economic growth, and a dedication to making education and literacy available to every citizen.

B. Americans have high expectations of progress and are eager to live up to their ideals.

C. This course will be descriptive of the American character, rather than prescriptive. The course will not argue that you need certain characteristics in order to be regarded as really American.

III. Americans over the last four centuries have exhibited a potent blend of practicality and idealism.

A. The practical can be divided into the areas of war, politics, and pioneering, although all three have an idealistic side to them.

1. War, for Americans, has always been a constructive matter. Warriors covered in this course include John Smith, Francis Marion, William Sherman, Edmund Ruffin, and Douglas MacArthur, whose life demonstrates that even the most powerful general can overstep the boundaries when he intrudes into the political realm.

2. Politicians will be represented by Thomas Jefferson in his role as an intellectual and Herbert Hoover as a humanitarian. American politics itself comes in many forms. In this course, we will look at the idealistic, yet shrewd and effective William Penn, founder of the colony of Pennsylvania; Abigail Adams, who linked the presidency with the idea of domestic harmony; and the water engineer William Mulholland, whose political maneuvering brought water to Los Angeles.

3. Our pioneers are subdivided into entrepreneurs and inventors, and explorers. They include Lewis and Clark, who represent American expansionism; John Wesley Powell, the first man to chart the Colorado River; the multitalented Benjamin Franklin; Eli Whitney; and Henry Ford, who perfected the art of mass production.

B. The idealists can be subdivided into artists, humanitarians, intellectuals, and religious figures.

1. Some figures, such as Leonard Bernstein and Duke Ellington are easily categorized as musicians.

2. Others are more difficult to place, such as Herbert Hoover, who was an effective humanitarian because of his practical and entrepreneurial skills.

C. Not all our characters were virtuous or likeable (though the course is biased heavily in favor of constructive rather than destructive men and women). Many seem to embody contradictions.

1. Edmund Ruffin was a passionate defender of slavery but also a talented agricultural scientist.

2. Andrew Carnegie was a ruthless businessman but also, in later life, a large-scale philanthropist.

3. Al Capone was a cold-blooded gangster who assassinated rival gangsters but claimed that he was a decent entrepreneur.

D. Several of the figures we will study were immigrants, but they adapted quickly to American habits, customs, and methods.

1. William Penn spent most of his life in England but introduced the principle of utopian community building in America, which lived on long after him.

2. Carnegie came from Scotland but soon learned American business methods in a way that outstripped nearly all his American-born rivals.

3. Samuel Gompers was an English Jewish immigrant who organized the American Federation of Labor.

IV. Americans have always been rigorous critics of themselves and have always struggled to live up to, and refine, their ideals.

   A. Few of the figures studied in this course were self-satisfied. Nearly all strove constantly to improve themselves and their society. American history is full of workaholics.

   B. They were more likely to test America against their ideals, and find it wanting, than to test it against the other nations in the world, and find much about which to congratulate themselves. Cotton Mather's Jeremiad tradition has persisted beyond Puritanism and become secularized.

V. National character may show recurrent characteristics, but that is not to imply that it is something perpetual and unchanging.

   A. Alexis de Tocqueville's comments on America are more than 150 years old, yet still relevant to many aspects of American life.

   B. Nevertheless, a society cannot be transformed from overwhelmingly rural to almost entirely urban, from poverty to wealth, without immense consequences for its people's outlook, attitudes, and beliefs.

   C. The challenge of historical study is to make the right distinctions between continuities and changes.

Essential Reading:

Kevin Phillips, *The Cousins Wars: Religion, Politics and the Triumph of Anglo-America*.

Alexis de Tocqueville, *Democracy in America*.

Supplementary Reading:

Richard Hofstadter, *The American Political Tradition and the Men Who Made It*.

Paul Johnson, *A History of the American People*.

David Potter, *People of Plenty: Economic Abundance and the American Character*.

Questions to Consider:

1. What are the benefits and drawbacks of the idea of "national character"?

2. Have the distinctive characteristics of Americans changed as society, culture, and technology have changed?

Lecture Two
John Smith—The Colonial Promoter

Scope: John Smith was the most important member of the Jamestown colony, England's first permanent settlement in what is now the United States. The most famous incident in his life was his rescue by the Indian princess Pocahontas, but he was also a talented soldier, explorer, mapmaker, and organizer, who probably did more than anyone else to prevent the colony from dying out in its chaotic early years. He was a writer, too, whose books about the first days of English colonization of North America provide one of the best sources we have about its problems and difficulties and about the misconceptions the English settlers had about this new land. In a sense, it is misleading to talk about Smith as an American—he never thought of himself as one and lived in the Americas for only about three years. On the other hand, he had many of the qualities that successive generations of Americans would also show, especially the explorers and soldiers. He rose to a position of leadership by his own exertions and gave a kind of premonition of the fluid social class system that America would create. It's also possible to see echoes of John Smith 200 years later in the transcontinental expedition of Lewis and Clark. Like them, Smith was boundlessly energetic, a close and accurate observer of human and animal life in a strange country, a good writer, and endowed with a cool nerve in confrontation with the Indians.

Outline

I.   Smith's adventurous early life prepared him for the challenges of the Virginia experiment.

    A. He was born in 1580 in Lincolnshire and enjoyed a good basic education.

    B. He traveled widely in Europe and the Middle East in his late teens and early 20s.

        1. He fought for the "Protestant cause" in the Netherlands in the 1590s.

        2. He fought for the Hungarians against the Turks.

3. Captured and sold into slavery, he killed a cruel master and escaped into southern Russia before making his way back to England.

C. He invested in the Virginia Company and accompanied the first expedition of 1606–1607.

II. Smith played a vital role in enabling the Virginia colony to survive.

   A. He explored the surrounding territory and contacted the local Indians.

   1. During an early exploration up the Chickahominy River, he was captured by Indians of Powhatan's confederacy.
   2. Struck by Powhatan's magnificence, he feared he would be sacrificed.
   3. According to a later version of the incident, though not his first account of it (*A True Relation*, 1608), Pocahontas intervened to save his life.
   4. Smith returned to the settlement, and Pocahontas later married another Virginia settler, John Rolfe.
   5. Smith's observations and writing about the Indians remain an excellent source for historians and anthropologists.

   B. Smith established work rules for the reluctant colonists.

   1. From ineptitude, laziness, or sickness, many of the colonists refused to plant food and do other necessary work to ensure their survival.
   2. Smith used a mixture of intimidation and diplomacy with the local Indians to get them to make up his own colony's deficit of food.

   C. He joined in the quest for the "northwest passage."

III. Smith spent most of the rest of his life writing about his Virginia adventures and trying, unsuccessfully, to return there.

   A. His departure after a severe accident in 1609 led to the catastrophic "dying time" in the colony, demonstrating his importance in its early welfare.

   1. A hundred miles upstream from Jamestown, on an exploring journey by canoe, Smith was badly burned and injured by the explosion of a gunpowder bag.

2. Subsequent events showed how necessary he had been to the colony. After he left, all but 60 of the 500 colonists died; some were forced into cannibalism to survive.

B. He kept in touch with developments in Virginia but never returned.

1. He published a big book on the colony, *A Map of Virginia* (1612), and compiled an anthology, *A Generall Historie of Virginia, New England, and the Summer Isles* (1624).
2. On a later voyage (in 1614), Smith explored parts of the New England coast.
3. He petitioned the Virginia Company to let him return there after an Indian uprising and massacre of the colonists in 1622.

C. Historians have disagreed about Smith's virtues and effectiveness. Although he took a keen interest in the Indians and their way of life, he never romanticized them and began a centuries-long policy of attempting to intimidate and dominate them.

Essential Reading:

Philip L. Barbour, *The Three Worlds of Captain John Smith*.

J. A. Leo Lemay, *The American Dream of Captain John Smith*.

Supplementary Reading:

John Smith, *Complete Works*, Philip L. Barbour, ed.

Alden T. Vaughan, *American Genesis: Captain John Smith and the Founding of Virginia*.

Questions to Consider:

1. Why were most of Smith's fellow colonists so unproductive?
2. How had Smith's earlier life prepared him for his work in Virginia?

Lecture Three
William Penn—The Religious Liberty Advocate

Scope: The last lecture examined a colonial pioneer, John Smith. William
Penn was a colonial pioneer, too, a proprietor who enjoyed a high
degree of control over Pennsylvania, the colony he founded. But
where Smith was a soldier, Penn was a pacifist, whose Quaker
beliefs inhibited him from fighting, even though he was born
during the English Civil War and lived in an age of almost
constant strife. He is one of the first great advocates for making
America a land of religious liberty, for permitting people of
different faiths to live and work together, letting every one
worship in his or her own way. Religious freedom, embodied in
the First Amendment to the Constitution, is so central to the
American way of life by now that it's difficult to recall what a
radical notion it once appeared. Penn was born in 1644 and lived
to 1718 and made only two short visits to Pennsylvania, from
1682–1684 and from 1699–1701. Like Smith, he would never
have described himself as an American, even though he has had a
lasting impact on this country's history. Again like Smith, his life
and work are shrouded in pious folklore, but we know enough
about him to be able to disentangle the real story from the myths.

Outline

I. Penn came from a distinguished political and military family and
remained politically influential throughout his life.

    A. His father, William Penn, Sr., was an admiral and a war hero of
Britain's commercial wars against the Dutch.

        1. In the interregnum, he served Oliver Cromwell, the Lord
Protector.

        2. Changing his allegiance at just the right moment, Penn was
able to win favor and a knighthood under the restored
Charles II.

    B. His son William was born in 1644 and enjoyed wealth and
privilege in childhood.

1. William studied briefly at Christ Church, Oxford, just after the Restoration, when John Locke, Christopher Wren, Richard Hooke, and Robert Boyle were working there.
2. His father sent him to a Protestant academy at Saumur in France, where he learned swordsmanship and courtly dress.
3. He briefly studied law at the Inns of Court as part of his preparation to lead his family and take responsibility for its estates.

C. William was strongly attracted to Quakerism on hearing the preaching of Thomas Loe in Ireland in 1667. His father, a senior courtier, was dismayed by his conversion to what was then regarded by Anglicans as an extremist sect.

II. From 1667–1682, Penn lobbied on behalf of tolerance for Quakers and other religious dissenters and suffered periodic imprisonment for his beliefs.

A. Memory of the recent Civil War-era upheavals made the Restoration Parliament eager to enforce religious uniformity. Penn was imprisoned in the Tower of London in 1668 and refused the bishop of London's plea for a change of heart.

B. Many of Penn's early writings, especially *The Great Case of Liberty of Conscience,* were appeals for religious toleration. He was imprisoned for illegal street preaching and for contempt of court in the famous Penn-Meade trial of 1670.

III. Pennsylvania was designed as a colony for Quakers and other persecuted Protestant groups, English, German, Dutch, Finnish, and Swedish, but it was also, from the beginning, a commercial proposition.

A. King Charles II granted Penn the colony partly in repayment of a debt owed to his father, who had died in 1670. He had earlier written a charter for Quaker settlers in New Jersey, which included a pledge of religious toleration.

B. Penn wrote promotional pamphlets extolling the colony's commercial and farming benefits. He sold many of the best lots in the projected city of Philadelphia to the wealthy Quaker merchants of the Free Society of Traders.

C. His "Frame of Government" went through several drafts and remained controversial among the settlers.

D. He visited Philadelphia in 1682, arriving just after his 38th birthday.

    1. Philadelphia was a model city, designed on a rational grid system between the Delaware and Schuylkill Rivers.

    2. Penn was determined to maintain better relations with the Indians than most of the other English colonies had.

    3. He faced constant political controversy with his council and assembly.

E. He was disappointed at the hard pragmatic turn that Philadelphia politics took almost at once.

IV. Penn had to struggle to maintain control of his proprietorship in subsequent decades.

    A. He became a principal advisor to King James II (1685–1688) in the hope of assuring religious freedom in Britain. James's disastrous reign and flight into exile discredited Penn.

    B. William III and Mary II, doubting Penn's loyalty after the Glorious Revolution, seized his colony in 1692. Penn was able to clear his name and regain the colony in 1694.

    C. He returned to Pennsylvania in 1699, stayed for two years, and witnessed the colony's rapid growth and prosperity.

        1. Because the climate was healthier than that of Virginia and the Carolinas, population grew rapidly, from immigration and natural increase.

        2. Like Virginia and Maryland, Pennsylvania used indentured servants and legalized slavery in 1700.

        3. On his second visit, Penn faced a challenge from the monarchy to take over direct control, because the proprietor's pacifism prevented him from adequately defending Pennsylvania's frontiers from Indian attack and its waterways from pirates.

    D. In 1708, Penn was defrauded by one of his trusted Quaker agents.

E. Pennsylvania, despite all its teething troubles and despite the disillusionment Penn felt over his inability to control its development, showed that religious freedom would work and that a colony could prosper without religious uniformity. It also showed that religious idealism would have to make its way in the midst of a commercial rapacity that could sometimes be very hard-hearted.

Essential Reading:

Mary Geiter, *William Penn*.

Harry E. Wildes, *William Penn*.

Supplementary Reading:

Joseph J. Kelley, Jr., *Pennsylvania: The Colonial Years*.

Catherine Owens Peare, *William Penn: A Biography*.

Questions to Consider:

1. What balance of practical and idealistic motives prompted the founding of Pennsylvania?

2. In what ways did Penn's ideas influence later events and changes in American history?

Lecture Four
Cotton Mather—The Puritan

Scope: John Smith and William Penn were Englishmen who had a big impact on America but spent most of their lives elsewhere. Cotton Mather, by contrast, was born in America and spent his whole life there. His name has become a byword for ferociously intellectual Puritanism at its most rigorous. He lived from 1663 to 1728 and was descended, on both sides of his family, from the leading Puritan ministers who had settled Massachusetts Bay in the 1630s. He tried to keep alive a spirit of religious rigor in Boston, a community that was becoming more complex and more worldly and one that seemed to have fallen away from the pious simplicity of its Puritan founders. He is famous for his role in the Salem Witch trials of 1692 and for introducing smallpox inoculations into Boston early in the 18th century. Historians of the colonial period of American history are often vexed by the lack of written sources available to them—there are many questions we would love to answer but cannot for lack of records. Cotton Mather is the great exception to this rule. He published more than 400 books and pamphlets, wrote thousands of letters, and kept a detailed diary in which he both described events and agonized over the condition of his soul. As a result, there are few Americans from any age whose lives, external and internal, we can follow in such close detail. Historians and biographers of Mather, with such a wealth of information at their disposal, have disagreed over how to understand him. To some, he represents Puritanism at it worst; to others, he is a sterling example of a dignified and thoughtful American adapting to his rapidly changing world.

Outline

I. Most of Cotton Mather's life was spent in the shadow of his powerful father, Increase Mather.

    A. Increase Mather was minister of the Old North Church in Boston.

    B. Cotton was the oldest of nine children born to Increase and his wife, Maria Cotton.

1. He showed exceptional intellectual promise as a child and graduated from Harvard at age 16.
2. As a teenager, he suffered from a stammer and feared that it might prevent him from following the family tradition of becoming a preacher.
3. He preached his first sermon at age 18, from his father's pulpit.

C. Increase Mather went to England on behalf of the colony in 1688 to try to restore its charter after the Glorious Revolution. Cotton, a newly ordained minister, was made anxious by having to run his father's affairs during the long absence.

II. Cotton was almost morbidly preoccupied with his sins, the destiny of his soul, and what appeared to him the declining religiosity and rising worldliness of his community.

A. He accepted the principle of predestination but sought for reassurance of his own salvation.
1. He wrote at length about his own sins, of sloth, pride, and lust.
2. He feared that his mind was not sufficiently attuned to God.

B. He was alarmed by the fact that a declining number of Bostonians experienced the conversion experience that the first generation of Massachusetts Puritans had believed essential to full church membership.
1. The *Halfway Covenant* of 1662 had been designed to adapt the church to this crisis.
2. Some ministers, such as Solomon Stoddard, wanted to abandon conversion as a criterion for church membership and admit all who desired to join.

C. Mather also deplored the fact that the ministry itself was declining in influence. He was a master of *jeremiads*, sermons lamenting community decline.

D. Mather was politically naïve, often misjudged prominent figures in public life, and developed passionate enmities.
1. Convinced that the cares of the whole Reformation lay on his shoulders, he tended to see opponents as demonic.
2. With increasing frequency, he compared himself to Christ and saw himself as a suffering martyr.

E. He preached the duties of children and parents to one another.

III. Cotton Mather struggled with old and new theories about the world.

A. He was 29 during the Salem Witch Hunt of 1691–1692.

B. Hysterical teenage girls in the community believed they had been bewitched by specters.

C. Local magistrates took the accusations seriously and convened a court, headed by Deputy Governor William Stoughton.

D. The court convicted 20 people and put them to death on the basis of specter evidence.

E. Mather shared the widespread belief that witches were real and that they were plaguing Salem, but he urged a higher standard of incriminating evidence.

F. His book, *Wonders of the Invisible World* (1693), justified the trials retrospectively.

G. As a contemporary of Isaac Newton, he had to come to terms with the idea of a universe moving according to uniform laws.

1. His father, by contrast, understood earthquakes, comets, storms, and epidemics as "special providences" sent by God as punishment for sins.

2. Cotton Mather held the two systems in uneasy mental balance but generally favored the new science.

3. Like Newton, he regarded gravity as God's instrument for maintaining uniform motion in the universe.

H. Improvements in astronomy and microscopy introduced Mather to immense and minute forms.

I. He took a practical interest in medicine and public health, advocating inoculations during a smallpox outbreak in 1721.

1. Mather's slave Onesimus told him about the practice in Africa, and he read reports of it being used in Turkey.

2. He urged Bostonians to try the method, and Zabdiel Boylston did so, experimenting on his son and two slaves, all of whom recovered.

3. Many Bostonians rebuked Mather for promoting what seemed to them an insane activity.

4. Some historians have hailed him as a pioneer of modern medicine, but others caution that his advocacy was, in its time, reckless.

IV. Puritanism contributed strongly to the American character.

    A. Its religious side persisted even while changing.

        1. Popular religion, especially after the Great Awakening, became more emotional and less intellectual.

        2. Theology remained, and has remained up to the present, a vigorous element of American intellectual life.

    B. Moral Puritanism persisted through subsequent centuries.

        1. It was apparent in the idea of the American revolutionary era that America must be a virtuous republic, free of European decadence.

        2. It undergirded antebellum reforms, such as abolitionism, and such later movements as Prohibition and, in our own era, political correctness.

    C. The heritage of Puritanism has been, and continues to be, contested.

        1. Admirers cite the Protestant work ethic.

        2. Detractors, including H. L. Mencken, regarded Puritanism as the worst element in America's heritage.

Essential Reading:

Robert Middlekauff, *The Mathers: Three Generations of Puritan Intellectuals*.

Kenneth Silverman, *The Life and Times of Cotton Mather*.

Supplementary Reading:

Perry Miller, *The New England Mind: From Colony to Province*.

Kenneth Silverman, ed., *Selected Letters of Cotton Mather*.

Questions to Consider:

1. Should we try to understand Cotton Mather by applying recent psychological theories to his behavior?

2. Would Massachusetts have benefited from Mather wielding greater political power?

Lecture Five
Benjamin Franklin—The Improver

Scope: One characteristic that Americans do *not* exhibit is fatalism. If something is wrong, they will fix it, and if something works slowly, they will speed it up. The whole of American history is full of people trying restlessly to improve their farms, their machines, their society, their culture, their relationships, and their entire way of life. None of America's improvers is more famous than Benjamin Franklin. Born in humble circumstances, son of a tallow chandler, he became one of the most famous men not only in America but equally in Europe, where his distinguished scientific career and his diplomatic service to revolutionary America brought recognition and honors. His life also showed that upward social and economic mobility was an American reality; Franklin was not only an improver but a self-improver, too.

Outline

I. Born and raised in Cotton Mather's Boston, Franklin's earliest publications were satires on Mather's busybody ways.

  A. The secular world that Mather dreaded was the one Franklin loved and helped to develop, and he early became disillusioned with Puritanism.

  B. Franklin came to believe that the most important thing in life was not to be assured of salvation but to be useful here on earth.

  C. He spent his early adulthood in Pennsylvania and, as a leader of the anti-proprietary party, became prominent in striving to undo William Penn's legacy.

  D. After 1757, he spent more time abroad, in Britain and France, than in America and was the first American to win widespread fame in Europe.

II. As a printer and writer, Franklin helped pioneer the most literate society in history.

  A. He was apprenticed to his older brother James, who founded Boston's first newspaper, the *New England Courant*.

B. Eager to write as well as to print, he wrote the anonymous "Silence Dogood" letters.

C. Denied advancement by his envious brother, Franklin ran away to Philadelphia.

    1. There, after early adventures and a trip to England to perfect his knowledge of the trade, he established himself as an independent printer.

    2. He made a fortune with *Poor Richard's Almanac.*

    3. His *Pennsylvania Gazette* improved the quality of the American press.

D. He founded Philadelphia's first library.

E. His extensive literary output is entirely secular.

    1. Like the Puritans, Franklin was concerned with morality but from a practical, secular point of view.

    2. His *Autobiography* explains the development of his philanthropic and enlightened outlook.

III. Franklin was a gifted amateur scientist and inventor.

A. He was more interested in applied science than pure theory.

B. His experiments with electricity led to his development of lightning conductors.

C. Firewood shortages in Philadelphia prompted his development of the Franklin stove.

D. His charting of the Gulf Stream benefited trans-Atlantic voyagers.

E. Problems with his own eyesight led to his invention of bifocals.

IV. Franklin was a central figure in his era's political history, first locally, then nationally.

A. As clerk of the Pennsylvania Assembly for 15 years, then as a member, he learned the issues and methods of colonial democracy. He worked against the Penn family proprietors to turn Pennsylvania into a Crown Colony.

B. Franklin represented Pennsylvania in London between 1757 and 1762 and again from 1764 to 1775.

    1. Other colonies, including Massachusetts, New Jersey, and Georgia, asked him to represent their interests also.

    2. He addressed Parliament in 1766 to explain American reception of the Stamp Act and urge its repeal.

3. He incurred the wrath of the British government by "leaking" the Hutchinson-Oliver letters.

C. He served on the committee to draft the Declaration of Independence.

D. He was America's ambassador to France, from 1776 to 1785.

    1. Lionized as a scientist and savant, Franklin also made the crucial diplomatic breakthrough of winning French aid to the American cause in 1778.

    2. He was one of the American signatories of the Treaty of Paris (1783), by which the war ended and America won British recognition of its independence.

E. His name and prestige lent legitimacy to the Constitutional Convention in 1787, of which he was the host.

F. His funeral in 1790 drew 20,000 mourners.

Essential Reading:

Benjamin Franklin, *Autobiography*.

Edmund Morgan, *Benjamin Franklin*.

Supplementary Reading:

Bernard Bailyn, *To Begin the World Anew: The Genius and Ambiguities of the American Founders*.

Walter Isaacson, *Benjamin Franklin, an American Life*.

Questions to Consider:

1. What qualities in his personality made Franklin so successful?

2. Why was he such a luminous figure to British scientists and French intellectuals?

Lecture Six
Francis Marion—The Guerrilla Soldier

Scope: Benjamin Franklin is honored as one of the Founding Fathers, and rightly. But the United States became an independent nation only because it won the Revolutionary War. Without military success, no arguments in justification of independence would have swayed the British government. Francis Marion, the "Swamp Fox," is one of the semi-legendary soldiers of the Revolutionary War, who preserved the possibility of American independence in one of the most treacherous campaigns of the war. In his mid-40s, after a relatively uneventful early life, Marion suddenly had thrust upon him the responsibility of organizing resistance to the British in South Carolina after the capture of Charleston in 1780. With only a handful of volunteers to command, he led a succession of daring raids against British and loyalist lines of communication, emerging from, then vanishing back into, the swamp country he had known all his life. His adversaries, General Cornwallis and Colonel Banastre Tarleton, learned to dread him, and he disrupted their plans for an advance into North Carolina. Throughout late 1780 and early 1781, Marion was at his most effective, until the arrival of a new American general, Nathanael Greene, enabled the regular army to resume operations. He was transformed from man into myth by Parson Weems, an early 19th-century patriotic biographer, who used him as an object lesson in teaching American children the nature of selfless service to their country.

Outline

I. By now, it is sometimes difficult to sort out the truth from the myth, but a study of Francis Marion's life is useful for showing the ugly reality of the revolutionary war in the South. It was a contest of acute uncertainty, with constant changing of allegiances among the frightened residents, mutual atrocities, and a deteriorating sense of civil restraint.

II. In the Revolutionary War, the American Continental Army was supplemented by militia and by guerrilla fighting.

A. Washington's experience had convinced him that a conventional field army was essential.

    1. Prolonged training and discipline were vital to battlefield success.

    2. He disliked militia soldiers after witnessing their lack of discipline and tendency to flee.

B. Washington kept the Continental Army in the field but won few battlefield engagements.

    1. Victory at Saratoga was attributable to a temporary American superiority in the field.

    2. Victory at Yorktown was attributable largely to French naval aid.

C. The work of the Continental Army was supplemented by militia and guerrilla fighting.

III. Marion's early life and experience prepared him to be an effective guerrilla fighter.

A. He was the youngest of six children, born in 1732 to a plantation owner on the Santee River in South Carolina.

    1. He went to sea as a 15-year-old but was shipwrecked.

    2. He took over management of his family's plantation at age 18, after his father's death.

B. Marion's military career began in the French and Indian wars. He distinguished himself as a militia lieutenant in fighting against the Cherokees.

C. After the war, he resumed life as a farmer, prospered, and bought Pond Bluff, a plantation of his own.

IV. Marion proved to be a superb soldier in regular engagements and in the small-scale engagements of the Revolutionary War in the South.

A. He spent the first four years of the war in Charleston with the Second South Carolina Regiment.

    1. He manned the Fort Sullivan artillery in June 1776 that drove off a British naval assault on Charleston harbor.

    2. He led part of the unsuccessful French-American attack on Savannah in 1779.

    3. A broken ankle prevented him from being in Charleston when British troops captured it in 1780.

B. Marion rallied South Carolinians, who were horrified by the repression of Charles Cornwallis and Banastre Tarleton.

    1. He began harassing raids on British and loyalist forces after Cornwallis's defeat of General Horatio Gates's Southern Army at Camden.

    2. With 50 militiamen, Marion liberated 150 prisoners, survivors of Camden, in a daring night raid and dispersed a Tory militia attack, despite odds of five to one against.

    3. Then, and in subsequent attacks on the British and loyalists, Marion took advantage of his knowledge of the densely forested and swampy terrain.

C. Cornwallis realized that he could not rely on the loyalty of nominal "loyalists" in South Carolina, especially when they were threatened by Marion's raids.

    1. In November 1780, he ordered Tarleton to track down Marion, but the attempt failed.

    2. The next month, Major Robert McLeroth, another British officer, challenged Marion to a mortal combat ordeal, with 20 soldiers on each side.

D. General Nathanael Green took over the southern department from General Gates and asked Marion to organize his espionage.

    1. He also asked Marion to continue raiding, to unnerve Cornwallis.

    2. Governor Rutledge appointed Marion general in command of the militia on New Year's Day 1781.

    3. He cooperated effectively with another revolutionary hero, "Lighthorse Harry Lee," but found it difficult to cooperate with "Gamecock" Sumter.

E. Marion's plantation was burned and in ruins when he returned to it at the end of 1782.

    1. The state gave him the role of commandant of Fort Johnson as a way of paying him and helping to relieve his debts.

    2. In 1786, aged 54, he married his 49-year-old cousin, the spinster Mary Esther Videau, whose wealth restored his fortune.

F. He served as a state senator and favored conciliation of former Tories.

V. After Marion's death in 1795, legends about him embroidered his historical accomplishments.

    A. Parson Weems was always willing to add fictitious elements to historical tales.

        1. He invented the story about Washington and the cherry tree, for which there is no historical basis.

        2. He used Peter Horry's account of his life with Marion and embroidered it to suit his didactic purposes.

    B. Marion's name became a byword for selfless patriotism.

        1. As the Weems version of Marion's life spread, thousands of parents named their sons Francis Marion.

        2. Twenty-nine towns and 17 counties founded after the Revolution were also named Marion.

    C. Irregular warfare and ingenious military improvisation characterized the expansion of America over the next century.

Essential Reading:

John W. Gordon, *South Carolina and the American Revolution: A Battlefield History*.

Hugh F. Rankin, *Francis Marion: The Swamp Fox*.

Supplementary Reading:

Peter Horry and Parson M. L. Weems, *The Life of General Francis Marion, a Celebrated Partisan Officer in the Revolutionary War*.

John Shy, *A People Numerous and Armed: Reflections on the Military Struggle for American Independence*.

Questions to Consider:

1. What role did Marion and other partisans play in the struggle for the hearts and minds of the South Carolina population?

2. Why was Marion able to outwit the British for so long?

Lecture Seven
Thomas Jefferson—The Patriot

Scope: Visitors from abroad are always impressed by Americans' intense pride in their own country. It was not always so. Throughout the colonial period, many Americans, including Benjamin Franklin through most of his life, liked to think of themselves as British. During and after the Revolution, however, a vivid sense of American national identity and patriotism developed quickly, as we saw in the case of Francis Marion in the last lecture. Thomas Jefferson lived from 1743 to 1826. He drafted the Declaration of Independence, was American ambassador to France during the French Revolution, and was the third president. His life has been scrutinized as carefully as that of anyone in American history, and you can spend years learning the details about his views on everything—not least because we still have literally thousands of his letters. For the purposes of this course on American character, however, we will view Jefferson mainly as an American patriot or nationalist. A striking aspect of American nationalism is its self-critical character, most apparent among the more highly educated Americans. Jefferson leads the way here, too, for he was not only proud of the United States and its revolutionary accomplishments but anguished about its imperfections, especially the blight of slavery. What's more, he was the living embodiment of a contradiction; idealizing equality as a fundamental aspect of the human condition, he kept slaves of his own. We all have feet of clay, and it's not surprising that Jefferson the man, as opposed to Jefferson the idealized hero, should have been contradictory and paradoxical. Hardly anyone in American history, or anywhere else, lives up to his or her own ideals. It's a shame, but it does not mean (as some of Jefferson's detractors believe) that we can, therefore, find nothing of lasting value in his life and work.

Outline

I. As a writer, Jefferson defended America's dignity and distinctiveness.

    A. His only published book, *Notes on the State of Virginia*, was largely an answer to an inaccurate and belittling French naturalist's account of the country.

        1. Comte de Buffon, a prominent French intellectual, claimed that American animals were smaller, feebler, and less numerous than those of the Old World.

        2. Jefferson, a gifted amateur scientist, described and championed America's landscape, flora, and fauna.

    B. The Declaration of Independence, which Jefferson drafted, has become the foundation of American identity. The Continental Congress chose him as draftsman because of his skill as a writer, exhibited earlier in *A Summary View of the Rights of British America* (1774).

    C. He took pride in his work for religious freedom, but in his religious skepticism, he was increasingly out of step with most of his contemporaries.

        1. He believed in religious freedom and ensured its accomplishment in Virginia.

        2. He denied that Jesus was divine, and his own version of the New Testament omitted all its supernatural elements.

        3. He had no sympathy with the evangelical revivalism that swept the post-revolutionary frontier.

II. Jefferson's personal life often contradicted his stated ideals.

    A. Favoring the simplicity of the yeoman farmer, he nevertheless lived luxuriously.

        1. For much of his life, he lived beyond his means and was in debt at his death in 1826.

        2. As American ambassador to France (after Franklin), he lived as ostentatiously as some of Louis XVI's courtiers.

    B. Jefferson's love of learning was more suited to men of leisure than to independent farmers.

        1. He founded the University of Virginia, chartered in 1819.

        2. The sale of his huge collection of books contributed to the foundation of the Library of Congress.

C. Deploring slavery, Jefferson nevertheless contributed to its preservation.
   1. He believed in intrinsic differences between the races.
   2. He wrote the new slave code for Virginia after the Revolution.
   3. Allegations of an affair with Sally Hemings have dogged Jefferson and his reputation ever since 1800.

III. As a politician, Jefferson's fortunes varied. He tried to promote a distinctive identity for the new nation but sometimes contradicted his own principles.

   A. As governor of Virginia, he was forced to flee from British cavalry in 1781.

   B. In the politics of the 1790s, he favored an agrarian republic of yeoman farmers against Hamilton's vision of a centralized commercial society. The Kentucky Resolutions of 1798, which he drafted, argued an extreme states rights position.

   C. Jefferson simplified protocol at the White House and made himself available to all visitors and correspondents. He paid postage on hundreds of citizens' letters and answered nearly all of them individually.

   D. Several of his policies as president violated his own principles.
   1. The Louisiana Purchase of 1803 almost certainly exceeded his constitutional prerogatives.
   2. His attack on the Barbary pirates relied on the navy, built under President Adams, that he had tried to forestall.
   3. The embargo of 1807 imposed hardships, especially on New England.

IV. His reputation shows immense flexibility.

   A. He died on July 4, 1826, the 50th anniversary of the Declaration of Independence and the same day as his old friend and rival John Adams.

   B. Groups with widely differing interests see Jefferson as their champion.
   1. Merrill Peterson wrote of *The Protean Jefferson* and Joseph Ellis describes him as *The American Sphinx*.
   2. The Confederacy honored him as a champion of states rights.

3. He still enjoys a high reputation as champion of religious freedom and as the man who put into words the reasons and justification for American independence.

Essential Reading:

Joseph Ellis, *The American Sphinx: The Character of Thomas Jefferson.*

Merrill Peterson, *Thomas Jefferson and the New Nation.*

Supplementary Reading:

R. B. Bernstein, *Thomas Jefferson.*

Garry Wills, *Inventing America: Jefferson's Declaration of Independence.*

Questions to Consider:

1. Why does Jefferson enjoy such a good reputation despite his many contradictions and despite the fact that he was a slaveowner?

2. What particular problems did Jefferson face as president in the opening years of the 19th century?

Lecture Eight
Abigail Adams—The First Lady

Scope: The subject of this lecture is Abigail Adams, one of America's first First Ladies, whose hundreds of surviving letters give us a vivid portrait of her character, her marriage, and her everyday life: in colonial Massachusetts (where she was born in 1744), in revolutionary America, at the courts of Europe, and in the new republic. She was a minister's daughter, devout, upright, moralistic, and full of the Yankee virtues of prudence, thrift, hard work, and sobriety. She was also widely read, strong-minded, and fascinated by the changing world around her and wrote a great deal about it to her husband, friends, and relatives. At a time when slavery existed throughout the United States, she was one of its early critics, and at a time when women had no political rights, she raised the possibility that a revolutionary nation might reconsider the idea. She was the first woman to live in the White House, when Washington, DC, was just a little building site in a forest clearing. Along with Martha Washington, she helped create the pattern that American First Ladies have followed throughout much of the last 200 years.

Outline

I.   Abigail Adams, born Abigail Smith, belonged to a distinguished Massachusetts family and enjoyed the conventional upbringing for a girl of her class.

   A. Her father was a Congregationalist minister, an important figure in the town of Weymouth.

   B. She was sick through much of her childhood and had no formal schooling.

   C. Her father was a learned man, however, and gave her and her two sisters a good basic education.

   D. She was wooed by John Adams from nearby Braintree, but her family was not sure that he, a farmer's son and a lawyer, was quite good enough for her.

   1. Nevertheless, they married in 1764.

2. They had five children, the second of whom, John Quincy (b. 1767) would later be secretary of state and president.

II. John Adams's rapid rise to political eminence kept him apart from his wife through much of the 1770s and 1780s, but his absences bequeathed to later generations their massive correspondence.

    A. John Adams was a leader among Massachusetts patriots and won Abigail's full support.

    B. While he was away, she witnessed the Battle of Bunker Hill from Penn's Hill nearby.

    C. When the United States declared its independence from British tyranny, Abigail reminded John, jokingly, that women might want to declare their independence from their domestic tyrants.

    D. She doubted whether Virginians, as slaveowners, could really be dedicated to liberty.

    E. She also argued that a virtuous republic would need to educate its girls as well as its boys.

    F. She became an effective manager of the family's lands and business.

        1. John Adams's services to the nation prevented him from gaining the fortune he would have acquired as a successful lawyer.

        2. Abigail became adept at renting houses and lands, importing and selling goods, and fending off the worst consequences of inflation.

III. After years of loneliness and anxiety in the Boston area, Abigail began to accompany John as he achieved seniority among America's leaders.

    A. She crossed the Atlantic in 1784 to join John in Paris, where he was negotiating postwar settlements and trade agreements. They had been apart for more than four years. Her description of the Atlantic crossing reminds us of how little we have to suffer as air travelers.

    B. Europe gave Abigail greater social poise and confidence than she had previously shown.

        1. Early experiences in France shocked her, but she gradually came to enjoy her time there.

2. Benjamin Franklin dismayed her, especially his flirtation with Madame Helvetius.
3. She found it difficult to deal with exiled loyalists, some of whom were homesick for Massachusetts, while others regarded the Adamses as traitors.
4. Despite her Puritan upbringing, she was fascinated by the theater but horrified by scantily clad dancing girls on stage.
5. She learned the self-discipline necessary to be a diplomatic hostess.

C. Abigail became skeptical about democracy and favored the federalists in the politics of the 1790s.
   1. She fell out with Jefferson, whom earlier she had greatly admired.
   2. As the vice-president's wife from 1788 to 1796, she enjoyed early years in New York and Philadelphia, the first two capital cities of the republic.

D. Abigail became First Lady when John Adams was elected president in 1896.
   1. She was the first female occupant of the executive mansion.
   2. Early experiences in Washington confirmed her dislike of slavery.

E. Her husband's defeat in the election of 1800 finally enabled the couple to live together in relative peace for the remaining years of her life.

IV. Abigail Adams helped shape the role of First Lady, now a venerable part of American tradition.

A. A First Lady must be loyal to her husband, represent the ideal wife and mother, and offer implicit but not explicit support for his policies.
   1. Jackie Kennedy played the role of fashionable, beautiful wife, yet dedicated mother.
   2. Edith Bolling Wilson became unpopular after her husband's stroke when she was accused of running the country.
   3. Hillary Rodham Clinton encountered severe opposition when she tried to advance one of her husband's most controversial initiatives directly.

B. A First Lady must represent a high moral tone.
  1. Mrs. Hayes, a prohibitionist, refused to serve alcohol at the White House.
  2. Eleanor Roosevelt became the living embodiment of liberalism during FDR's presidency and after his death.
  3. Hillary Clinton broke all precedents by undertaking an independent political career of her own after leaving the White House.

Essential Reading:

L. H. Butterfield et al., eds., *The Book of Abigail and John: Selected Letters of the Adams Family.*

Lynne Withey, *Dearest Friend: A Life of Abigail Adams.*

Supplementary Reading:

Charles W. Akers, *Abigail Adams: An American Woman.*

David McCullough, *John Adams.*

Questions to Consider:

1. Is it reasonable to think of Abigail Adams as a predecessor of modern feminism?

2. What aspects of Abigail Adams's life made it decisively different from those of subsequent First Ladies?

Lecture Nine
Mother Ann Lee—The Religious Founder

Scope: Religious innovation is one of the most distinctive aspects of the American identity. For 400 years, faith in unconventional religions has been a leading motive of migration to America, and for almost as long, new religions have been invented and developed here. Ann Lee, a near contemporary of Abigail Adams, was the principal figure in the creation of the Shakers. After years of persecution in England (persecution she brought on herself by deliberate provocation), she brought her closest followers to America in the hope that her strange new faith would win converts in the New World. After six years of neglect and adversity, her communitarian form of Christian millennialism began to attract New Englanders. Her premature death in 1784 could not prevent its spread in the following decades, even though its demand for absolute celibacy meant that no one would ever be born to Shaker parents and that recruits would have to accept and live a life of heroic self-discipline. Of all the people we will study in this course, Mother Ann Lee is the only one who never learned to read and write; all we know of her was written by others, and even more than with most historical characters, it is sometimes necessary to be skeptical about the stories she inspired.

Outline

I. Radical Christianity transformed the life of poor, illiterate Anne Lees of Manchester.

    A. She was born in 1736 but not baptized until 1742.

    B. Her father, John Lees, was a blacksmith.

    C. As a teenager, she heard and was profoundly influenced by George Whitefield, the great revival preacher who had mesmerized America.

    D. In 1758, she joined Jane and James Wardley's spiritual group, known as the "Shaking Quakers."

        1. They had no definite liturgy but relied on the Holy Spirit taking over their bodies.

      2. American newspapers heard of the group before any of its members emigrated to the New World.

  E. Ann Lee married Abraham Standerin, a blacksmith, in Manchester Cathedral in 1762.

      1. Neither of them could write, and they signed the register with crosses.

      2. Ann gave birth to four children in four years, but all died, which she interpreted as a judgment on her sinfulness.

  F. She came to believe that she represented the second coming of Christ.

  G. She now believed herself divinely protected.

II. Rising to leadership of the Shakers, Lee suffered persecution and eventually decided to move the group to America.

  A. Outspoken members of the group denounced all other forms of Christianity, sometimes breaking up Anglican services.

  B. In prison after one such incident, Lee enjoyed a vision of the future in America.

  C. With seven leading followers and financial help from a wealthy member, John Hocknell, Lee emigrated in 1774.

      1. She worked as a servant in New York City; her husband, as a blacksmith.

      2. Hocknell bought an estate northwest of Albany, New York, at Watervliet—then called Niskayuna.

  D. This group of English visionaries, suspected locally of opposing the Revolution, made little headway at first.

  E. In 1780, the Shakers began to make converts by encouraging visitors to watch their ecstatic worship.

      1. The famous "dark day," May 19, 1780, triggered their proselytizing.

      2. All who wanted to become members had to confess to Lee or one of her two male "elders" all the sins of their lives up to that point.

      3. Witnesses were fascinated by the Shakers' shouting, dancing, and spontaneous worship.

      4. Stories of Lee's power as a miraculous faith healer also spread.

III. The Shakers enjoyed success between 1781 and Lee's death in 1784 on a long recruiting tour through New England.

    A. Settling for several weeks at a time in different towns, they would model the example of their community life.

        1. The small town of Harvard, Massachusetts, became a second center for the group.

        2. Critics whipped the Shakers out of town in 1781, accusing them of being traitors to the Revolution.

    B. The conversion of James Meacham, a powerful Baptist preacher, helped the spread of the Shaker gospel.

    C. Lee reassured Meacham that she was not trying to revolutionize gender relations.

    D. Lee died unexpectedly in 1784, just seven weeks after death of her brother Father William Lee, her first convert and closest spiritual partner.

    E. James Whittaker, the surviving "elder," moved the group to New Lebanon, New York, and helped it adapt to new circumstances.

    F. Shakerism continued to spread, creating an idealized memory of Ann Lee.

IV. Upstate New York's "burned-over district" witnessed the birth of numerous other new versions of Christianity in the ensuing decades.

    A. The Assemblies of God, the Mormons, the Millerites, and the Oneida Perfectionists all originated in the area.

    B. Belief in human perfectibility and the imminent end have continued to inspire religious founders down to recent times.

    C. Shaker communities developed a successful form of Christian communitarianism and became famous for distinctive styles of design, architecture, and furniture.

Essential Reading:

Richard Francis, *Ann the Word: The Story of Ann Lee.*

Stephen Marini, *Radical Sects of Revolutionary New England.*

Supplementary Reading:

Edward Deming Andrews, *The People Called Shakers.*

John T. Kirk, *The Shaker World: Art, Life, Belief.*

Questions to Consider:

1. What made Ann Lee convincing to so many people?
2. How did the Revolution contribute to heightened religious enthusiasm in the 1770s and 1780s?

Lecture Ten
Rittenhouse and Bartram—The Scientists

Scope: In the second half of the 20th century and right up to the present, the United States led the world in scientific research and achievements. American funding, laboratories, and official support for the most complex research schemes were unparalleled. Every ambitious scientist from the rest of the world sought a permanent job, or at least a postdoctoral fellowship, at one of the major American research centers. This scientific leadership was in its infancy in the 18th century and relied on gifted amateurs and individualists. Recognition in those days had to come from European centers, and increasingly, after 1750, it did come. We have already seen a scientific side to the work of Franklin and Jefferson, men whose names we remember mainly for their political achievements but who were also enthusiastic and gifted amateur scientists. Less well known today, but famous in their own times, were David Rittenhouse (1732–1796) and William Bartram (1739–1823), the first, an astronomer, and the second, a prominent naturalist, who were among America's first professional scientists. Both came from Philadelphia, knew each other, and were friends of the era's revolutionary leaders.

Outline

I.   David Rittenhouse was lionized in colonial and revolutionary Philadelphia as an astronomer and instrument-maker.

    A. Born in 1732 at Norriton near Philadelphia, he became a clock maker and surveyor of colony and, later, state lines.

        1. He built high-quality clocks, telescopes, theodolites, compasses, and optical lenses.

        2. He charted the transit of Venus across the sun in June 1769.

    B. Rittenhouse built what was then the world's finest orrery.

        1. Rival colleges competed to buy it.

        2. Many admirers regarded it as the greatest miracle of the age.

        3. During the Revolution, Jefferson wrote Rittenhouse that he ought not to waste his energy on politics—science was more important.

C. Rittenhouse led a distinguished academic career.
1. At Penn, he was first professor of astronomy, then vice-provost, then a trustee.
2. He succeeded Franklin as president of the American Philosophical Society in 1791 and was appointed to the British Royal Society in 1795.

D. He was also director of the United States Mint from 1792–1795.

II. William Bartram explored the interior of Georgia and Florida and identified dozens of new plant, bird, and butterfly species.

A. His father, John Bartram, a Pennsylvania farmer, had an appointment to King George III as a specimen gatherer.
1. A friend of Benjamin Franklin in Philadelphia, John was one of the original members of Franklin's American Philosophical Society and founded America's first botanical garden.
2. William was the 7th of John's 11 children, and was born in 1739.
3. Father and son together explored the southeastern colonies in 1765.

B. William set off in 1773 to gather more as-yet-unknown and useful plants.
1. He had proved unsuccessful in farming and business but now had English patrons to cover his costs.
2. On a journey that lasted four years, he traveled across the Carolinas, Georgia, Florida, and the regions that are now Alabama, Mississippi, and Louisiana.

C. Bartram was unfazed by mosquitoes, alligator attacks, and other hazards.

D. His energetic and colorful writing brought remote areas alive to readers.

E. His *Travels* (1791) became an American classic, famous on both sides of the Atlantic.
1. He believed that the natural world gave evidence of God's benign design.
2. He personified rivers, plants, and animals.
3. He even included action sequences in his writing to describe the work of fly-trap plants.

F. Bartram witnessed a natural world of incredible abundance and diversity—including fish runs so thick that they seemed to create an almost solid surface on the river.

G. His book also shows him to have been an excellent ornithologist, and his catalogue of 215 American bird species was then the most comprehensive ever made.

H. In later life, Bartram was quiet and reclusive.

1. He declined an invitation to become professor of botany at the University of Pennsylvania in 1782.

2. Nearly all the senior American revolutionaries knew and admired him.

III. Both Bartram and Rittenhouse influenced later generations of scientists and writers.

A. America did not become the world leader in astronomy until the 20th century, when it could best afford massive telescopes, such as Mount Palomar and the Hubble telescope.

B. Many prominent botanists, herpetologists, ornithologists, and geologists retraced Bartram's trail and built on his observations.

C. Bartram was also admired by Coleridge and Wordsworth, who drew on his rich imagery.

Essential Reading:

William Bartram, *Travels and Other Writings*, Thomas Slaughter, ed.

Brooke Hindle, *David Rittenhouse.*

Supplementary Reading:

Edward Cashin, *William Bartram and the American Revolution on the Southern Frontier.*

Edward Ford, *David Rittenhouse: Astronomer and Patriot.*

Questions to Consider:

1. What practical difficulties confronted 18th-century scientists that their successors no longer need to consider?

2. What was the relationship between these scientists and the political crisis of the Revolution?

Lecture Eleven
Eli Whitney—The Inventor

Scope: One of the strongest and most distinctive aspects of the American identity has always been Americans' ability to make practical new devices and put them to profitable use. Another stereotype is that of the shrewd Yankee businessman who knows how to drive a hard bargain. Eli Whitney was an inventor and a businessman, but his greatest invention, the cotton gin, was almost too useful, and the bargain he tried to drive was almost too hard. The success of the cotton gin gave plantation slavery a new lease on life and prevented it from dying out, as had seemed possible at the end of the Revolutionary War. Southern planters found the gin so indispensable, however, that almost from the beginning, they refused to honor Whitney's patents, pirated his invention, and prevented him from making the immense fortune he had at first confidently anticipated. He undertook an exhausting round of lawsuits   litigation being another venerable element of the American way of life—and made limited headway in the effort to get paid. He next tried to make a fortune as a mass-producer of muskets for the government but found this endeavor unexpectedly difficult. He is, nevertheless, an important figure in shaping 19th-century America. His advocacy of mass production, if not his actual accomplishment of it, promoted the *American system* throughout antebellum America.

Outline

I. Born in Westborough, Massachusetts, in 1765, Whitney was exceptionally gifted in both practical and theoretical sciences.

A. He grew up tinkering in his father's workshop.

B. His formal education was delayed for lack of funds.

C. He saved money and made a good reputation as a schoolteacher in Grafton, Massachusetts.

D. In his mid-20s, he enjoyed a distinguished student career at Yale.

II. The cotton gin was a vital technical breakthrough but brought Whitney immense financial, technical, and legal troubles.

A. He devised it at Mulberry Hill plantation, under the patronage of Phineas Miller and Catherine Greene.
   1. According to folklore, Whitney got the crucial idea from watching a cat scratching a chicken.
   2. One man could clean 50 times as much cotton in a day operating a Whitney gin than he could working by hand.
B. Back in New England, Whitney perfected a model gin and applied successfully for an exclusive patent.
C. Thomas Jefferson corresponded with Whitney and asked whether a household-sized gin could be made for Monticello.
D. Whitney and Miller's unwise business plan tempted southern planters to copy the idea right from the beginning.
   1. The partners claimed one pound of cleaned cotton as payment for every five brought to them.
   2. They would probably have been wiser to sell licenses to manufacture gins, because they could not meet the demand.
E. Southern slave codes and an imperfection in the patent law made it difficult to convict violators.
   1. The slaves who operated the gins were not permitted to testify in court.
   2. Whitney and Miller had to lobby the federal government to modify the wording of the 1793 patent law, after which they began to win some cases.
   3. In 1802, the legislature of South Carolina voted Whitney and Miller $50,000 for the rights to the machine.
F. By 1820, slave cotton farming was spreading westward rapidly. Cotton became America's biggest export.
G. The American South and British cotton mills formed a mutually beneficial relationship.

III. Whitney's *American system*, applied to the manufacture of firearms, standardized and speeded up production methods.
A. Whitney confirmed in practice what Adam Smith had declared in theory—that the subdivision of labor leads to more efficient mass production.
B. In 1798, Whitney offered to provide 10,000 identical muskets to the U.S. Army.

1. He understood the theoretical benefits of interchangeability and hoped to realize it in practice.
2. His contract assured him an advance of $10,000 and an open credit line with the federal government.
3. He built a factory at East Rock, Connecticut; hired workmen; and set to work but encountered countless technical difficulties.
4. In January 1801, he impressed the outgoing and the incoming presidents with an exhibition of his musket locks' interchangeability.

C. Fears of an imminent war with France in 1798 had led President Adams's administration to award the contract and successive administrations to accept Whitney's delays.
   1. We now know that many other manufacturers were making muskets at the same time by similar methods.
   2. When the federal government job was finished, Whitney won comparable contracts from New York and Connecticut to make arms for their state militias.

D. The muskets did not work very well.

E. Whitney was often sick and grumbled incessantly about ill health.
   1. He married in 1817 at age 52.
   2. He died in 1825 after a long and painful illness.

IV. Despite his practical problems, Whitney's impact on American industrialization was profound and long-lasting.

A. He is a central figure in the history of the American system of manufacture.

B. His work had long-term significance on both sides of the Mason-Dixon Line.

Essential Reading:

Constance Green, *Eli Whitney and the Birth of American Technology*.

David Hounshell, *From the American System to Mass Production*.

Supplementary Reading:

David Noble, *Forces of Production: A Social History of Industrial Automation*.

Merritt Roe Smith, "Eli Whitney and the American System of Manufacturing," in *Technology in America: A History of Individuals and Ideas*, Carroll W. Pursell, ed., pp. 45–61.

Questions to Consider:

1. Which was more important in the long run, the cotton gin or the American system of manufacturing, and why?

2. Do you find Whitney to have been an admirable character?

Lecture Twelve
Lewis and Clark—The Explorers

Scope: In an earlier lecture, we saw how President Jefferson bent the constitutional rules when he seized the opportunity of buying the Louisiana territory from France. Lewis and Clark, a pair of army captains, led the Corps of Discovery on a three-year mission. Their job was to map the territory, to see whether it would provide an easy route to the West Coast and the Pacific Ocean for trade with Asia, and to gain American control of the lucrative trans-Mississippi fur trade. The two captains worked well together and lost only one of their 33 men, despite Indian attacks, sickness, and bouts of near starvation. They brought back to the president a vast trove of information about the American West's geography, flora, fauna, and peoples. Their industriousness as observers and collectors and their self-discipline in the face of human and natural threats assured the expedition's success. They laid the foundations of the nation's subsequent westward expansion.

Outline

I. Lewis and Clark's early experiences prepared them for their demanding expedition.

    A. Lewis, an army officer, was President Jefferson's near neighbor in Virginia and had become his private secretary.

    B. Clark, also a Virginian, had been an army officer and Lewis's commander in the Whiskey Rebellion.

II. The expedition followed major waterways across the American West.

    A. Lewis began by sailing down the Ohio River from Pittsburgh to its junction with the Mississippi.

    B. From St. Louis, the expedition followed the Missouri westward, then north to what is now North Dakota.

        1. Lewis and Clark established firm discipline by court-martialing delinquents.

        2. They sought treaties with Indians whom they met en route, and they spent the winter of 1804–1805 with the Mandans.

3. Among the recruits who joined them that winter were Charbonneau and his Indian wife, Sacagawea, with their newborn son, Jean-Baptiste.

C. Progress was impeded in early 1805 by natural and human obstacles.

    1. The Rocky Mountains proved far higher and more extensive than the explorers had hoped.

    2. The Great Falls of the Missouri compelled them to abandon their boats and proceed on foot.

    3. Choosing the route at river junctions became increasingly difficult.

    4. Meeting and communicating with the Shoshone Indians was facilitated by Sacagawea.

D. A hard mountain crossing and descent of the Snake and Columbia Rivers eventually brought the expedition to the Pacific Ocean.

E. The explorers spent the winter of 1805–1806 at the Pacific, in uneasy cohabitation with the local Indians.

F. The long journey back was punctuated by further adventures.

    1. Lewis shot and killed a Blackfoot Indian when a group of them tried to steal the explorers' guns.

    2. Lewis was accidentally shot by another of the men, Pierre Cruzatte, when they were out hunting elk.

    3. Arriving back in St. Louis, they found they had been away so long that they were assumed dead.

    4. Back in Washington DC, Lewis and Clark were awarded land grants of 1,600 acres each by Congress in recognition of their service to the nation.

III. Their later lives mark a dramatic contrast.

A. Clark became commander of the Louisiana militia and, later, Superintendent of Indian Affairs at St. Louis.

    1. He did everything he could for Sacagawea, whose help had been crucial among the Shoshones.

    2. He created an early museum of Native American artifacts.

B. Lewis, always morose and inclined to depression, became an incurable alcoholic and died within three years of the expedition's return.

IV. Subsequent western explorers built on the achievements of Lewis and Clark.

    A. Zebulon Pike explored the southern plains to the Rockies and predicted that the land would remain uninhabitable because of its lack of trees.

    B. John Wesley Powell, whom we will encounter later in this course, was the first man to explore the Grand Canyon by boat, in a venture of comparable daring.

Essential Reading:

Stephen Ambrose, *Undaunted Courage.*

Landon Y. Jones, ed., *The Essential Lewis and Clark.*

Supplementary Reading:

David Lavender, *The Way to the Western Sea: Lewis and Clark across the Continent.*

James Ronda, *Lewis and Clark among the Indians.*

Questions to Consider:

1. What factors contributed to the success of Lewis and Clark's expedition?

2. Why were the Corps of Exploration's relations with Native Americans often fraught with conflict and strained?

Lecture Thirteen
Charles Grandison Finney—The Revivalist

Scope: In the first part of the course, we studied prominent men and women in colonial and revolutionary America as they created a new nation and began to expand its boundaries. In this second part, we'll single out people who transformed the new republic in the years between the Revolution and the Civil War. The United States spread rapidly westward, with settlers lured by the availability of land and believing that it was America's "manifest destiny" to occupy the entire continent from sea to shining sea. In the South, this expansion was fueled by a demand for cotton that could be grown by slave labor then ginned on Eli Whitney's machine before being exported to England. In the North, a free-labor economy turned progressively against slavery, foreshadowing the terrible conflict of the 1860s.

These Americans were confident, assertive, entrepreneurial, and by comparison with their European counterparts, highly educated. They were also fervently religious and thrived on evangelical revivals. Charles Grandison Finney (1792–1875) is, deservedly, one of the most famous evangelists in American history. Taking up a tradition begun by George Whitefield in the colonial era, he reshaped it to suit the expansive commercial society of the early 19th century. He emphasized free-will conversion and taught a brighter theological message than the gloomy old Calvinists. He also became a central figure in Christian education and in the movement to abolish slavery. Unlike Cotton Mather, who was a pillar of his community, and unlike Ann Lee, who expected the apocalypse to take place at any moment, Finney combined a challenge to social and religious conventions with a realistic appreciation of how Christians should live their daily lives.

Outline

I. Finney was raised in the "burned-over district" of upstate New York and suffered religious uncertainty until his conversion.

A. His parents were not ardently religious.

B. He found the preaching of uneducated ministers unconvincing.

C. He trained as a lawyer in Adams, New York (1818–1821), and would have had a successful career as an attorney.

D. Sudden conversion to Christianity in 1821 made him resolve to switch careers and become a minister.

    1. Finney's conversion story is an American evangelical classic.

    2. He told a client the next day: "I have a retainer from the Lord Jesus Christ to plead his cause. I cannot plead yours."

    3. Becoming a Presbyterian minister, he was dismayed by the Calvinist harshness of his church's Westminster Confession.

II. Finney's preaching style drew in thousands of converts but also provoked disapproval and controversy from the established Protestant ministry.

A. An imposing figure at 6 feet, 2 inches, with piercing blue eyes, he adopted theatrical mannerisms in the pulpit; he magnetized and browbeat audiences.

B. His theology emphasized free-will conversion rather than passivity.

    1. He used the "anxious bench" to focus attention on struggling sinners.

    2. He permitted women to pray in public and particular sinners to be prayed over by name.

    3. In *Lectures on Revivals in Religion* (1834), he explained how revivals could be organized and denied that they were miraculous.

C. Lyman Beecher (father of Harriet Beecher Stowe) and other eastern leaders denounced Finney but were unable to halt his revivals' success.

    1. They condemned the turbulence of Finney's revivals, which appeared to threaten social hierarchy.

    2. They noted that exuberant converts were likely to fall away after the revival's excitement had passed.

D. Early successes in western New York State were matched by triumphant revivals in Philadelphia, New York City, and Rochester; the Rochester Revival (1830) electrified and transformed the entire city.

E. The rising business classes were particularly susceptible to Finney's approach. His influence spread with the support of Arthur and Lewis Tappan, wealthy businessmen and brothers who converted to his cause in 1832.

F. Finney preached for three years in New York, from 1832 to 1835.

III. Finney spent his mature years at Oberlin College as a professor, president, and antislavery advocate.

A. Oberlin was an Ohio college for training ministers in "new measures" of the sort Finney approved.

1. Funded largely by the Tappans, it was America's first coeducational college and the first to be racially desegregated.
2. Finney worked there from its opening in 1835 and was president from 1851 to 1866.

B. The Lane Seminary rebellion brought in large numbers of antislavery students.

1. At Lane in Cincinnati, students had been forbidden to debate slavery, and 93 out of 100 had left in protest, led by Theodore Weld.
2. Thirty-two of them transferred to Oberlin, making it an antislavery center from then on.

C. Finney was also a Congregationalist minister there from 1837 to 1872.

D. He continued to preach widely throughout America and ran successful revivals in England in the early 1850s.

IV. Finney probably did more than any other individual to create the shape of revivalist evangelicalism for the ensuing century or more.

A. Subsequent figures who followed his lead included Dwight Moody, Billy Sunday, and Billy Graham.

B. The revival tradition can still be glimpsed today at the political parties' nominating conventions.

C. Finney linked a powerful religious mood to the antislavery and other reform causes in antebellum America.

Essential Reading:

Richard Dupuis and Garth Rosell, ed., *The Memoirs of Charles G. Finney.*

Keith J. Hardman, *Charles Grandison Finney: Revivalist and Reformer.*

Supplementary Reading:

William G. McLoughlin, *Charles Grandison Finney to Billy Graham.*

G. Frederick Wright, *Charles Grandison Finney: American Religious Leader.*

Questions to Consider:

1. What made Finney's revival preaching more persuasive than that of his predecessors?

2. How did Finney's gospel correspond to political changes in the new republic?

Lecture Fourteen
Horace Mann—The Educator

Scope: In the previous lecture, we saw that in his later years, Charles Finney was a college president. So, too, was Horace Mann, one of the central figures in American educational history. No American characteristic is more striking to outsiders, including me, than the nation's dedication to education. The historian Richard Hofstadter once wrote a book called *Anti-Intellectualism in American Life*, but by comparison with most countries in the world, America has a rich educational and intellectual tradition. Moreover, American education has not been just for a tiny elite but for everyone—it is one of the most inspiring aspects of democracy at work. Mann himself, raised in humble circumstances on a New England farm, became secretary of the State Board of Education in Massachusetts in 1837. Idealistic, hard-working, pious, determined, and politically shrewd, he created, over the following 15 years, the first statewide public school system in America. It became a model for public school systems in all the other states and laid the foundations of today's system of universal education for all.

Outline

I. Mann was an ambitious farm boy who rose by dint of hard work, stern morality, and self-discipline.

   A. He was born in 1796 in Franklin, Massachusetts.
      1. A very short school year and an untrained teacher prompted him to rely on self-education from books.
      2. He rebelled against Calvinism and became a Unitarian.

   B. He graduated from Brown University in the class of 1819 and studied for the bar at Lichfield Law School.

   C. His law practice in Dedham, Massachusetts, founded in 1823, prospered and led to his election to the General Court (state assembly) in 1827.

II. Mann excelled as a state politician and administrator.

    A. He was named secretary of the State Board of Education in 1837.

        1. He encountered a school system in decay, starved of money, and an educational law that was widely ignored.

        2. Through wide travel, speaking, lobbying, and legislative reforms, he created the first statewide universal compulsory educational system in America.

        3. By the time he left the job, after 12 years, he had laid the foundations of universal compulsory schooling for all Massachusetts children.

    B. Mann created America's first *normal school*, for the training of teachers, at Lexington in 1839.

    C. His 12 masterful reports to the state government embody his philosophy of education.

        1. The reports urged the necessity of a curriculum that corresponded to the students' later lives and their rights and responsibilities as citizens.

        2. The Seventh Report urged emulation of good German methods.

    D. Mann argued for a Christian but nondenominational approach to religious instruction.

    E. He had to face constant opposition to almost every element of his program.

        1. Farmers were reluctant to lose their children's labor to an extended school calendar.

        2. Taxpayers resented having to pay for better school buildings, teachers, books, and normal schools.

        3. He faced the accusation of "Prussian" centralization.

        4. Members of many denominations objected to the generalized Christianity he proposed.

III. In 1848, Mann took over the recently deceased John Quincy Adams's seat in the House of Representatives.

    A. He was an outspoken congressional opponent of slavery.

    B. He accepted appointment as president of the new Antioch College, Yellow Springs, Ohio, in 1852.

1. The school was not finished when he arrived but had the appearance of a construction site.
2. Disastrously mismanaged by its founders, it staggered through the 1850s constantly on the brink of bankruptcy.
3. Mann's own prestige and sympathetic Unitarian supporters back East enabled it to survive.

C. Other states and other nations' governments consulted him about establishing public educational systems; he was much admired in Britain, for example.

IV. The public school system has been a foundation of American prosperity ever since Mann's era.

A. Americans are suspicious of state-funded welfare schemes but free public education is itself an example of such a scheme.

B. Mann certainly did not foresee the vast array of problems that would later beset public school systems.

C. The schools successfully Americanized generations of immigrants.

Essential Reading:

Robert Bingham Downs, *Horace Mann: Champion of the Public Schools*.

Jonathan Messerli, *Horace Mann: A Biography*.

Supplementary Reading:

Ernest Freeberg, *The Education of Laura Bridgman*.

Mary Tyler Peabody Mann, *Life of Horace Mann*.

Questions to Consider:

1. What qualities and circumstances made Mann such a successful educational reformer?

2. Did Mann's antagonists have any strong arguments, or was he sure to win on the merits of his case?

Lecture Fifteen
Ralph Waldo Emerson—The Philosopher

Scope: Ralph Waldo Emerson (1803–1882) was a close contemporary of Charles Grandison Finney and Horace Mann. His similarities to them and his differences from them are equally striking. He is famous as the leading figure among the Transcendentalists, an idealistic group of philosophical and social radicals in pre-Civil War New England. His lectures and essays made him the most famous American thinker of his era, at home and in Europe. Dissatisfied with the old New England Puritanism, Emerson was also impatient with the Unitarianism that had displaced it and that proved a lifeline for Horace Mann. That doesn't mean he accepted Finney-style evangelicalism. Instead, forsaking all the conventional Christian doctrines, he proposed a radically individualist religion, a direct contact between the believer and God, with no intermediaries. As Emerson told it, the individual was more likely to encounter the divine reality during a stroll in the woods than during a church service.

Outline

I. Emerson planned to follow his father's footsteps into the ministry but found he lacked the conviction to be a conventional minister.

    A. Born in 1803, he was educated at the Boston Latin School and at Harvard.

        1. Graduating in the class of 1821, he finished only 30th in a class of 53 students.

        2. He taught school with his brother William before attending Harvard Divinity School.

        3. Illnesses, which may have been psychosomatic, interrupted his studies.

    B. Ordained in 1829 and called to Boston's Second Church, Emerson was a conscientious but uninspired minister.

        1. His wife, Ellen Tucker Emerson, died in 1831, only two years after their marriage.

        2. He resigned his ministry in 1832.

C. After a long visit to Europe, he began his career as a traveling lecturer.

    1. Josiah Holbrook had founded the Lyceum Movement in 1826, creating suitable venues in the growing western cities.

    2. Emerson kept careful journals and filled them with finished paragraphs, which he would then assemble into lectures and essays.

    3. His advocacy of individualism and personal initiative found a sympathetic hearing in such settings.

II. Emerson broke new philosophical ground in the late 1830s.

    A. *Nature* (1836) denied the sharp separation of humanity and the natural world, arguing that they were all elements of the same thing, united in thought.

    B. The Phi Beta Kappa Address at Harvard (1837), "The American Scholar," urged American scholars to create a style and idiom of their own and not to be stifled by European and traditional models.

    C. The Divinity School Address (1838) condemned Unitarianism, along with all other forms of "historical" Christianity.

        1. It caused a press scandal.

        2. Emerson's *Essays* (1841) answered his critics by reasserting the supremacy of the individual soul over authority, tradition, and Scripture.

    D. Emerson argued that society must make room for its intellectuals.

III. The Transcendentalists had a variety of theoretical and practical interests and an enthusiasm for experimentation.

    A. Philosophically, they were idealists, in reaction against materialism.

        1. Transcendentalism was part of the Romantic reaction against Enlightenment rationalism and the new utilitarianism.

        2. Religiously, the Transcendentalists were almost pantheistic.

    B. They experimented with utopian communalism at Brooke Farm but could not persuade Emerson to join in.

    C. Thoreau, Emerson's friend, took some of his ideas to their logical extremes.

        1. *Walden* demonstrated Thoreau's belief that most men worked too hard and neglected their surroundings.

2. Thoreau acted on his antislavery principles by going to prison rather than paying taxes that would support the pro-slavery Mexican War.

IV. Emerson, aloof from politics in his early career, gradually became a passionate antislavery advocate.

    A. Advocating radical individualism in the 1830s and 1840s, he doubted the wisdom of social reform movements and philanthropy.

    B. A successful lecturing tour of Britain in 1847 enhanced his fame, making him, in effect, a celebrity-intellectual.

    C. He honored John Brown as a martyr to the cause of abolition and was an ardent Union man during the Civil War.

V. By the post-Civil War years, Emerson had become a national institution.

    A. Harvard, which he had antagonized in the 1830s, gave him an honorary doctorate and made him a trustee in the late 1860s.

    B. Memory loss slowed his powers after 1870.

    C. The other Transcendentalists recognized his influence over them.

Essential Reading:

James Elliot Cabot, *A Memoir of Ralph Waldo Emerson.*

Ralph Rusk, *The Life of Ralph Waldo Emerson.*

Supplementary Reading:

Ralph Waldo Emerson, *The Spiritual Emerson: Essential Writings*, David Robinson, ed.

Perry Miller, ed., *The Transcendentalists: An Anthology.*

Questions to Consider:

1. What did Emerson mean by *individualism*, and how did his definition differ from other American definitions of the term?

2. Why was Emerson so popular, despite his unusual and iconoclastic views?

Lecture Sixteen
Frederick Douglass—The Abolitionist

Scope: The first 15 lectures in this course on American identity have all been about white men and women, nearly all of them with British ancestry. But they lived in a nation full of African-American slaves. Some of them, especially members of the revolutionary generation who said they were fighting for liberty, had bad consciences about building their republic of liberty on the backs of slaves who could never be free. By the 1830s, a growing number of influential Americans, including Charles Grandison Finney and Horace Mann, believed slavery to be so wrong that it should be abolished at once. Emerson joined the abolitionist chorus in the 1850s, by which time the movement had found an eloquent spokesman in Frederick Douglass, a former slave who had escaped from bondage. His moving autobiography and his electrifying oratory energized abolitionists in the 1850s and helped precipitate the crisis of the union. The first African-American to become famous in Europe, he advised President Lincoln during the Civil War and led the struggle for freedmen's rights at the war's end.

Outline

I. Born Frederick Bailey on a Maryland plantation in 1818 to a slave mother and an unknown white father, Douglass learned early the degradation of slave life.

   A. On the plantation of a man who may have been his father, he and the other slave children were fed cornmeal mush from a trough.

      1. Inadequately clad for winter, they slept in a huddle for warmth.

      2. He witnessed the brutal flogging of slaves, including his aunt.

   B. Moving to Baltimore at age 9, with his master's married daughter, Sophie Auld, Douglass enjoyed better treatment and learned how to read.

      1. Sophie's husband prevented the lessons, which violated Maryland law.

      2. Douglass experienced an emotional religious conversion at the age of 13.

C. Sent back to the plantation as a teenager, he was brutally beaten by a "slave-breaker" named Edward Covey and swore to escape from slavery.

    1. His first escape attempt, in 1836, was discovered, but he got away from a Baltimore shipyard on his second attempt, in 1838.

    2. He changed his name and settled in New Bedford, Massachusetts, but discovered that even in the North, racial prejudice was widespread.

II. Douglass became an internationally famous writer and speaker on behalf of abolition.

    A. He met William Lloyd Garrison, editor of the *Liberator*, in 1841, and they became mutual admirers.

        1. Douglass made his first public speech on the issue at Nantucket in 1841 and showed a superb oratorical skill.

        2. He accepted an appointment as a lecturer for the Anti-Slavery Society.

    B. He wrote his *Narrative* and published it in 1845, with subsidies from sympathetic abolitionists, including Horace Mann.

        1. His sincere Christian faith gave added point to his condemnation of slavery.

        2. He was acclaimed in Britain and Ireland during an 1846–1847 lecture tour.

    C. Moving to Rochester, New York, Douglass published *The North Star*, an antislavery newspaper, beginning in 1848.

        1. He advocated self-help and self-advancement for the free black population.

        2. He advocated votes for women.

    D. He took a middle position between Garrison's pacifism and John Brown's advocacy of antislavery insurrection.

        1. Passage of the Fugitive Slave Act in 1850 radicalized Douglass.

        2. He participated actively in the Underground Railroad, sheltering escaped slaves and sending them on to Canada.

        3. He joined first the Liberty Party, then the Republican Party, in search of a political end to slavery.

E. He tried to dissuade John Brown from attacking Harper's Ferry in 1859; implicated in the raid, Douglass had to flee to Canada to escape arrest.

III. During and after the Civil War, Douglass continued to agitate for abolition, then for freedmen's constitutional rights.

    A. His journal urged free northern blacks to enlist in the Union army.

        1. He persuaded more than 100 men from upstate New York, including his two sons, Lewis and Charles, to join the army.

        2. He met with Lincoln and other Republican government leaders, who recognized him as an African-American community leader and assured his position.

    B. A Republican Party stalwart, he served in a series of political jobs after the war.

        1. He was marshal and recorder of deeds for Washington, DC, in the 1870s and early 1880s.

        2. He represented the United States as ambassador in Haiti in 1889–1891.

    C. Douglass's marriage to a white woman, Helen Pitts, in 1882, caused controversy.

Essential Reading:

Frederick Douglass, *The Narrative of the Life of Frederick Douglass.*

Philip S. Foner, *Frederick Douglass.*

Supplementary Reading:

David B. Chesebrough, *Frederick Douglass: Oratory from Slavery.*

Douglas T. Miller, *Frederick Douglass and the Fight for Freedom.*

Questions to Consider:

1. What decisions did Frederick Douglass have to make in advancing the abolitionist cause?

2. Why was northern opinion divided on the question of emancipating the slaves?

Lecture Seventeen
Edmund Ruffin—The Champion of Slavery

Scope: Frederick Douglass was a passionate opponent of slavery. Edmund Ruffin (1794–1865) was an equally passionate advocate of slavery, so dedicated to its existence and so horrified by its eventual overthrow that he greeted Confederate defeat in 1865 by committing suicide. He represented the old white southern culture of racial supremacy, had a touchy and easily inflamed sense of honor, and became one of the uncompromising "fire-eaters" who defended slavery, then secession, then the Confederate States of America, to the bitter end. But what makes Ruffin a fascinating part of American history and a contributor to the American identity was his skill as an agricultural scientist. He has been referred to as the father of scientific agriculture. Recognizing early in life that southern farming techniques, especially tobacco and cotton cultivation, depleted the soil, he argued for a wide array of new agricultural practices. He wanted to be sure that the South would continue to prosper and that the economic basis of the slave system might not be undermined. As a soil scientist, Ruffin seems very modern, but as a pro-slavery advocate, he seems utterly irrelevant and abhorrent to our world. American history is full of dramatic contradictions, though they are rarely met in such acute forms as they are with Edmund Ruffin.

Outline

I. Born and raised in Virginia, Ruffin early recognized that southern agriculture, as currently practiced, was unsustainable.

 A. On Coggin's Point, his inherited Tidewater estate, he found that depleted acidic soils responded well to treatment with alkaline "marling."

  1. His technique required a rigorous, scientifically disciplined approach, accurate measurement, and scientific knowledge from all farmers.

  2. It was labor-intensive and required consolidated farms and large labor forces.

 B. Ruffin published "An Essay on Calcareous Manures" in 1832.

C. He edited the *Farmer's Register* from 1833–1842. Like Frederick Douglass with the *North Star*, he found it difficult to make a profit from running his journal.

D. Governor Hammond of South Carolina appointed Ruffin Agricultural and Geological Surveyor of that state in 1843. He made a detailed survey of the state and continued to advocate improved farming methods but found most planters reluctant to change their ways.

E. He spent much of the 1840s at Marlbourne, a new farm on the Pamunkey River, which he marled, drained, and made fertile and productive.

II. Ruffin came to believe that slavery was not merely a tolerable evil but a positive good.

A. As a young man, he had doubted the rightness of slavery.

    1. He intervened on behalf of a black man wrongly accused of joining Nat Turner's revolt in 1831.

    2. Articles in early editions of his journal argued for colonization.

B. As abolitionist rhetoric intensified, Ruffin was one of many southerners whose pro-slavery convictions hardened.

    1. Ruffin argued that without the protection offered by slavery, the inferior black race would go into decline, suffering, and extinction.

    2. He repeated other pro-slavery advocates' observation that slavery was not condemned in the Bible.

C. A "fire-eater," along with Robert Rhett and William Yancey, Ruffin began to urge secession in the 1850s.

    1. He believed that secession was constitutional.

    2. He feared that the antislavery forces in Congress would prohibit its spread to the territories, thereby confining slavery to the southeast and outvoting it.

    3. He feared that abolitionists would foment slave rebellions.

    4. He believed that secession was a way to prevent war.

III. Sixty-five years old when Lincoln was elected, Ruffin agitated for secession and fought to the end in the Confederate army.

A. He took part in early engagements of the war, though already 67 years old.

1. He fired one of the first shots at Fort Sumter.
2. He witnessed the first Battle of Bull Run in the summer of 1861.

B. His farms were overrun and plundered by Union troops during the war, and his slaves scattered or enlisted into the Union army.

C. He carefully planned and committed suicide in 1865.

Essential Reading:

David F. Allmendinger, Jr., *Ruffin: Family and Reform in the Old South*.

William Mathew, *Edmund Ruffin and the Crisis of Slavery in the Old South*.

Supplementary Reading:

Betty L. Mitchell, *Edmund Ruffin: A Biography*.

James Oakes, *The Ruling Race: A History of American Slaveholders*.

Questions to Consider:

1. Was Ruffin right in thinking that his proposed agricultural reforms for the South could work only with the help of slavery?

2. What were the strongest arguments for slavery and against it, from the point of view of southern slaveowners themselves?

Lecture Eighteen
Brigham Young—The Religious Autocrat

Scope: The slavery question became increasingly urgent in mid-century America, as the examples of Frederick Douglass, Edmund Ruffin, and the abolitionists Horace Mann and Charles Grandison Finney demonstrate. But slavery was not the only issue provoking intense passions. Another was the rapidly growing Mormon church. It had been founded at the end of the 1820s in the religiously volatile "burned-over district" of upstate New York by a farm boy named Joseph Smith. Brigham Young (1801–1877) was one of its early recruits and suffered repeated bouts of persecution with the early church. When Smith was lynched in 1844, Young became the Mormons' second and greatest leader. Abandoning the United States altogether, he led almost the whole Mormon population on a spectacular transcontinental journey into the area we now call Utah, but which was then a scantily inhabited part of Mexico. Centralizing nearly all decisions in himself, Young transformed desert land into irrigated farms, kept strict control over every aspect of the community's life, and became the area's territorial governor after America's war with Mexico brought Utah into the Union. The Mormons, even in this remote setting, were not immune to persecution, because their custom of polygamy horrified and scandalized public opinion in the rest of the United States. Young himself was a leading practitioner of polygamy and had 27 wives.

Outline

I. Young rose to prominence among the early Mormons as Joseph Smith's most reliable lieutenant.

    A. Born in Vermont and raised in the "burned-over district" of upstate New York, he struggled to find a good livelihood.

        1. His family migrated out of the harsh Vermont country but found no easy success around the Erie Canal.

        2. Under the influence of his brothers and in the midst of the Second Great Awakening, he became a Methodist.

B. Young and his entire family committed themselves to the new Mormon sect in 1832, and he at once became an ardent preacher and missionary.

C. Shortly after this group conversion, Young's wife, Miriam, died of tuberculosis, but Young remarried, to Mary Ann Angell, with whom he had six children.

D. A meeting with Joseph Smith at Kirtland, Ohio, prompted Young to pray in tongues.

    1. Smith began to advance Young in the church, appointing him a member of the Quorum of Twelve.

    2. When the Mormon settlement in Far West, Missouri, was persecuted by pro-slavery settlers, Young participated in a rescue mission with "Zion's Camp."

E. Young took over temporary leadership during Smith's imprisonment in 1839 but relinquished it at once when Smith returned.

    1. When the Missouri settlement was overrun in 1838, with Governor Lilburn Boggs's complicity, Young organized evacuation and eastward migration to Nauvoo, Illinois.

    2. Despite recurrent crises and poor health, Young regularly traveled in the East and to England in a successful search for further recruits.

    3. Young married his first plural wife in 1842.

F. Joseph Smith's assassination in 1844 led to Young's promotion.

    1. Smith was killed at Carthage, Illinois, while Young was preaching in New England.

    2. Returning, Young ruled with the Twelve and managed the completion of the Nauvoo Temple.

II. The Mormons' Great Trek was a brilliant accomplishment and soon became part of the Latter Day Saints' mythology.

A. In February 1846, Young led 16,000 emigrants over the Mississippi and across Iowa to Winter Quarters (now Florence, Nebraska).

B. The following year, he led an advance party to the Great Salt Lake and declared it the Latter Day Saints' new home.

C. He returned to Winter Quarters to supervise the large-scale migration that ensued in 1848.

1. Young appointed himself governor of the state of Deseret.
2. The Treaty of Guadelupe-Hidalgo (1848) made the Utah territory part of the United States.
3. President Fillmore appointed Young governor of the Utah territory and superintendent of Indian affairs in 1851.
4. The Perpetual Emigrating Fund facilitated continuing migrations into Salt Lake City from the East and from Europe.

D. Young's tight, centralized control facilitated urban development and the major irrigation projects that made farming possible.

E. Mission journeys continued to seek recruits throughout the rest of America and abroad.

III. The United States' rapid transcontinental growth and the Mormons' persistence with polygamy inflamed relations between the two.

A. Appointment of a non-Mormon governor in 1857 almost led to war.
1. Tensions over the army's approach contributed to the Mountain Meadows massacre in September 1857.
2. Negotiations prevented bloodshed, but the army stayed nearby until 1861.

B. Young participated actively in the region's technological development in the 1860s and 1870s.
1. Mormons helped build the transcontinental telegraph line after 1861.
2. Mormon construction crews also worked on the Union Pacific/Central Pacific railroad link in 1866–1869.
3. Young promoted all-Mormon producer- and retail-cooperatives to ensure prosperity and economic welfare among Mormons and exclude the Gentiles.

C. At Young's death in 1877, the Mormon community faced a crisis over its retention of polygamy.

D. After 1890, the Mormons transformed themselves into paragons of social conservatism and American patriotism.

Essential Reading:

Leonard Arrington, *Brigham Young: American Moses.*

Richard Ostling and Joan Ostling, *Mormon America: The Power and the Promise.*

Supplementary Reading:

Newell Bringhurst, *Brigham Young and the Expanding American Frontier.*

Lee Nelson, ed., *A Prophet's Journal: Brigham's Young's Own Story in His Own Words.*

Questions to Consider:

1. Why were anti-Mormon sentiments so violent, and how did Young react to them?

2. What factors contributed to the success of the Utah migration?

Lecture Nineteen
Frederick Law Olmsted—The Landscape Architect

Scope: Brigham Young's life shows us a nation growing rapidly westward, crossing and settling the entire continent as the 19th century progressed. The life and work of Frederick Law Olmsted (1822–1903) also bear witness to a nation being rapidly transformed. He was the first American landscape architect, maker of large urban parks to alleviate the congestion and monotony of America's fast-growing cities. His most famous work, still there for all to see, is Central Park in New York, which he designed and built between 1857 and 1861. It made him famous and was the first of dozens that his company designed between that time and his death in 1903. Olmsted, another hard-driven Yankee like Eli Whitney, Horace Mann, and Charles Grandison Finney, was also, like them, an abolitionist. His writings about conditions in the slave South, where he traveled in the early 1850s, provided ammunition to Frederick Douglass, William Lloyd Garrison, Harriet Beecher-Stowe, John Brown, and other antislavery advocates. Landscape architecture and antislavery advocacy appear to have little in common. As Olmsted saw them, however, the two were connected, because each contributed to fulfilling his ideal of a society in which citizens were free, educated, genteel, and able to maintain contact with rural conditions. He had definite ideas about what the American identity should be and did everything he could to realize them.

Outline

I. Olmsted's education was unsystematic and erratic but endowed him with American idealism and a love of the countryside and the picturesque.

   A. Schooled by a variety of New England clergymen, he rejoined his family for regular vacations in search of the "picturesque."

   B. An episode of severe sumac poisoning prevented him from going to college and afforded him several years of unsystematic outdoor exploration and travel.

C. Olmsted resolved to show that farming, science, and civility were compatible.

D. Like Edmund Ruffin, he argued for a scientific approach to agriculture, showing that decayed farmland could be rejuvenated.

E. A walking journey in England inspired him with ideas for improving America; at Birkenhead, he saw Joseph Paxton's public park and took it as inspiration for his own later work in park design.

F. A series of expeditions to the slave South as correspondent for the *New York Times* led to authoritative books on the area; Olmsted explained in detail the inefficiency, as well as the inhumanity, of slavery.

II. An invitation to supervise the construction of New York's Central Park set the direction of Olmsted's life from 1857.

A. A wide array of urban problems became critical as cities expanded and industrialized; lack of any contact with the countryside for working people jarred against American rural traditions.

B. Olmsted and Calvert Vaux submitted the winning design, "Greensward," for the project; the site—wasteland, dumps, and pigsties—seemed unpropitious.

C. Olmsted's practical knowledge and administrative skill enabled him to supervise the transformation of vision into reality.

III. He played a crucial role in the U.S. Sanitary Commission during the Civil War.

A. Differences with the park commissioners had prompted many trial resignations from the park.

B. Olmsted proved a capable executive secretary of the U.S. Sanitary Commission.

    1. It was a semiprivate organization, created in the early ad hoc days of the war, but it won President Lincoln's approval.

    2. It feuded against the Army Medical Bureau.

C. Jurisdictional disputes caused Olmsted to leave the Sanitary Commission in 1863.

D. He spent two years on the California frontier at the Mariposa estate.

IV. He and Calvert Vaux resumed their partnership and the administration of Central Park after the Civil War; they used this position as a springboard to working nationwide on other park projects.

    A. They took on and defeated New York's notorious "Boss" Tweed in 1871.

    B. Olmsted designed parks for Chicago, Buffalo, Boston, Atlanta, Montreal and Washington, DC.

        1. He transformed the Boston Fenway from a reeking slum into an "emerald necklace" of parks.

        2. He designed the landscaping around the U.S. Capitol building in Washington, DC.

        3. He laid out the campus of the new Stanford University.

        4. He planned a park on the site of the 1893 World's Fair in Chicago.

    C. Olmsted helped the fledgling national park idea become a reality, designing facilities at Yosemite and Niagara Falls.

Essential Reading:

Witold Rybczynski, *A Clearing in the Distance: Frederick Law Olmsted and America in the Nineteenth Century*.

Elizabeth Stevenson, *Park-Maker: A Life of Frederick Law Olmsted*.

Supplementary Reading:

Charles E. Beveridge and Paul Rocheleau, *Frederick Law Olmsted: Designing the American Landscape*.

Albert Fein, *Frederick Law Olmsted and the American Environmental Tradition*.

Questions to Consider:

1. Do the many aspects of Olmsted's life and career genuinely complement one another?

2. What made Olmsted's parks so admirable and successful in the eyes of generations of Americans?

Lecture Twenty
William Tecumseh Sherman—The General

Scope: The last soldier we examined, Francis Marion, specialized in lightning guerrilla warfare in the South Carolina low country of the Revolutionary War. William Sherman, by contrast, represents what later became the characteristic American style of warfare, bringing overwhelming force against the enemy and battering it into submission. He is one of the most controversial people in American history, still widely admired by soldiers for his military effectiveness and as one of the two men who broke the long deadlock of the Civil War. For white southerners, on the other hand, especially those seduced by romantic Confederate memories, Sherman is one of the great villains of American history, who, by burning and smashing everything in his path during his notorious "march to the sea," introduced a savage form of total war to the South.

Outline

I. Sherman's early hopes of military glory were disappointed.

    A. Orphaned at the age of 9, he was brought up by the Ewings, a nearby family headed by a U.S. senator from Ohio.

    B. Sherman studied at West Point and graduated 6th in a class of 43.

    C. Hoping for action in the Mexican war, he was shipped instead to California.

    D. He married Ellen Ewing, whom he had known since childhood; left the army; and worked as a banker, first in California, later in Kansas.

    E. His bank, on Montgomery Street in San Francisco, has survived repeated earthquakes and still stands.

    F. Sherman headed a military academy in Louisiana but resigned when Louisiana seceded and the Civil War began.

II. The outbreak of the Civil War in 1861 first gave Sherman the opportunity to put his military training into practice, and he rose quickly on merit.

A. He distinguished himself as a cool-headed artillery commander at the first Battle of Bull Run, a Union defeat.

B. He understood the importance of restoring order and morale after this humiliation.

C. Commanding federal troops in Kentucky in the late summer of 1861, he became convinced that he was outnumbered and briefly suffered a nervous breakdown.

D. Subsequently, he became General Grant's most trusted subordinate and began to develop his theory of total warfare.

    1. Shiloh (1862) was the first battle in which Sherman made a superior impression.

    2. He recognized that "war is hell" but also that he was good at it.

    3. He paid tribute to the skill and daring of his adversaries, especially the cavalry.

    4. He contributed to the Union victory at Chattanooga in 1863.

III. Grant entrusted Sherman with the advance from Chattanooga to Atlanta in the summer of 1864.

A. If the campaign had failed, Lincoln could easily have lost the election of 1864.

B. Sherman tried to avoid frontal assaults and failed when he tried one at Kennesaw Mountain, northwest of Atlanta.

C. He besieged Atlanta and took the city in August 1864, when the Confederate Army withdrew to prevent complete encirclement.

D. He argued in favor of marching to the Atlantic coast, devastating enemy resources. Savannah surrendered to him in December 1864.

E. The ensuing campaign in South Carolina was logistically more difficult but equally destructive.

    1. Joe Johnston surrendered to Sherman in Raleigh, North Carolina, in April 1865.

    2. Back in Washington, Sherman participated in the Grand Review, an immense parade of the victorious Union armies.

IV. Sherman's destructive campaigning, then and subsequently, has remained controversial.

A. Sherman was widely hated in the South for his destructiveness but equally widely admired in the North for bringing the war to an end by the application of extreme measures.

B. Subsequent American campaigns have borne his stamp.

C. Appointed General of the Army by President Grant in 1869, he declined to meddle in politics.

Essential Reading:

Stanley Hirshon, *The White Tecumseh: A Biography of General William T. Sherman*.

William T. Sherman, *Memoirs*, Charles Royster, ed.

Supplementary Reading:

Anne J. Bailey, *War and Ruin: William T. Sherman and the Savannah Campaign*.

James M. McPherson, *Battle Cry of Freedom: The Civil War Era*.

Questions to Consider:

1. Was Sherman's harsh policy in Georgia and South Carolina justifiable?

2. What were the benefits and drawbacks of Sherman's non-political approach to the war?

Lecture Twenty-One
Louisa May Alcott—The Professional Writer

Scope: General Sherman soon learned that war was hell. So did Louisa May Alcott (1832–1888), daughter of one of the Concord Transcendentalists, who volunteered as a nurse in a Civil War hospital. Horrified by scenes of suffering, mutilation, and death and the hospital's filthy environment, Alcott succumbed to typhoid fever and almost died. For the rest of her life, she suffered from mercury poisoning because of the medicines she had been given during that crisis. Despite these hardships, she became a prolific novelist and one of the two or three most widely loved children's authors in American history. *Little Women*, a fictional transfiguration of her own childhood, became a classic almost at once and has remained one ever since its publication in 1868.

Outline

I. Louisa's father, Bronson Alcott, had unusual and impractical ideas that made her childhood difficult but also highly unusual and stimulating.

   A. His educational theories were idealistic and paid insufficient attention to children's real nature or to community prejudices. An experimental school he ran was forced to close when he admitted a black student, causing all the white children's parents to withdraw them.

   B. He tried to make a living giving "conversations" but spent as much money traveling to them as he earned from them. His circle of friends (and, therefore, Louisa's) included Emerson, Thoreau, Longfellow, and Hawthorne.

   C. His experiment in communal vegetarian living, "Fruitlands," lasted only two years.
      1. Louisa's book *Transcendental Wild Oats* tells its story.
      2. She tried to discipline her wild instincts, to be submissive and patient.

II. With her three sisters and her mother, Louisa Alcott early set about trying to sustain the family economy.

A. Her early jobs included reading aloud to an old couple, doing laundry, teaching elementary students, mending clothes and dolls' clothes, and performing domestic service.

B. She wrote plays and a newspaper in the family, then began trying to make money by selling stories and poems.

   1. Many of Alcott's early works were pseudonymous and have only recently been recognized and collected as hers.

   2. She was an enthusiastic supporter of the abolitionist cause.

   3. Her sister Lizzie died of scarlet fever in 1856 at the age of 23 (she was to be the model for Beth in *Little Women*).

C. Alcott's stint in a Union hospital in Washington, DC, proved disastrous to her health but gave her new insights that were later turned to literary effect.

   1. The nurses were organized by Dorothea Dix, humanitarian and friend of Horace Mann.

   2. Alcott's duties were exhausting and stressful.

   3. She became critically ill and was dosed with calomel.

   4. She made a slow recuperation at home.

D. *Hospital Sketches* widened her literary reputation.

III. *Little Women* made her nationally famous and salvaged the family's fortunes.

A. The novel creates an idealized version of its author's own childhood.

   1. It has generated psychoanalytical speculation among critics.

   2. As her fame grew, Alcott came to be included among the literary celebrities on whom her father lectured, along with Longfellow, Emerson, Hawthorne, and Thoreau.

B. All her subsequent books were guaranteed good publicity and wide sales.

C. Her health suffered from the mechanics of writing and from residual effects of the calomel.

   1. Generating copies in a pre-Xerox era required high-pressure writing.

   2. Alcott learned to write with her left hand, as well as her right.

D. She outlived her domineering father by only two days, dying in 1888.

IV. Alcott was one of the women who dominated American fiction in the second half of the 19th century.

   A. Before the Civil War, Harriet Beecher Stowe had made a sensation with *Uncle Tom's Cabin* (1852).

   B. Elizabeth Stuart Phelps's *The Gates Ajar* (1867) was another postwar sensation.

   C. Nathaniel Hawthorne, whom Alcott knew, was impatient with women writers but could not match their success.

   D. Alcott's books remain popular, and several were made into movies during the 20th century; *Little Women* was the basis for two silent films and three talkies, from 1933, 1949, and 1994.

Essential Reading:

Martha Saxton, *Louisa May: A Modern Biography of Louisa May Alcott*.

Madeleine Stern, *Louisa May Alcott, A Biography*.

Supplementary Reading:

Louisa May Alcott, *Little Women*.

Elizabeth Keyser, *Whispers in the Dark: The Fiction of Louisa May Alcott*.

Questions to Consider:

1. Was Alcott trapped by Victorian conventions about a woman's role in society, or did she benefit from them?

2. Did her unconventional childhood and difficult adolescence help or hinder her development as a writer?

Lecture Twenty-Two
Andrew Carnegie—
Conscience-Stricken Entrepreneur

Scope: General Sherman led Union soldiers into battle and Louisa May Alcott tended the wounded. Meanwhile, the Union advanced to victory largely because of its economic superiority. Frederick Law Olmsted had said that the South was economically stagnant and backward, and travelers who had visited both sections nearly all agreed. By the time of the Civil War, on the other hand, the northern economy was in high gear and going at full speed through the stages of the industrial revolution. After the war, the economic expansion accelerated further, while a handful of larger-than-life business leaders became wealthy and powerful on a previously unimaginable scale. Among them was the iron and steel manufacturer Andrew Carnegie (1835–1919). Not content with building an immense business empire and piling up wealth for its own sake, like many of his successful contemporaries, Carnegie also became a leading philanthropist and a kind of amateur economic philosopher—his "gospel of wealth" influenced generations of Americans and suggested an uneasy conscience behind the complacent rhetoric.

Outline

I. Born poor in Scotland, Andrew Carnegie found economic opportunity in the United States.

    A. His father, a handloom weaver, was a victim of industrialization.

    B. The family migrated to Alleghany, Pennsylvania, in 1848.

    C. Among his early jobs, Carnegie worked as a textile factory hand, messenger, and telegrapher.

    D. He became clerk to Tom Scott of the Pennsylvania Railroad, and their careers rose together.

II. As a businessman on his own account, Carnegie showed outstanding ability.

A. Rising rapidly in railroad management, he switched to full-time investment at the end of the Civil War.

B. He gained a powerful position in the steel industry, which made him a multimillionaire.

    1. From 1865 to 1872, he was principally an investor and speculator.

    2. In 1872, he decided to concentrate exclusively on the steel industry.

    3. He had learned valuable entrepreneurial and management skills from the railroads.

    4. He modernized equipment constantly and made high-quality steel rails.

    5. He pioneered in vertical integration, acquiring iron ore mines, coal mines, Great Lakes steamers, and his own railroad.

C. Workers faced brutal conditions and a grueling 12-hour day.

D. Carnegie was ruthless in suppressing trade union opposition. In the Homestead Strike of 1892, he and his deputy, Henry Clay Frick, starved the Amalgamated Association of Iron and Steel Workers into submission.

E. Businessmen enjoyed high social prestige in the late 19th century.

    1. Carnegie, Rockefeller, Vanderbilt, J. P. Morgan, and others were often lauded as the "captains of industry."

    2. The mightiest of them all, especially those who attempted to monopolize, were vulnerable to the accusation that they were "robber barons."

    3. Early on, Carnegie had expressed doubts about the dignity of mere money-getting but, in practice, found it almost irresistible.

III. Carnegie became a writer, philosopher, and philanthropist.

    A. In "The Gospel of Wealth" (1889), he argued that rich men held their fortunes in trust and should use them wisely to aid the less fortunate.

        1. He emphasized that donations should be socially useful but should not be charity, which sapped independence and will.

        2. In *Triumphant Democracy* (1886), he praised the era's outstanding economic accomplishments.

    3.   Influenced by Darwin and Herbert Spencer, he came to believe that his success was "natural."

B.   Carnegie founded and endowed free libraries in America and Britain.

C.   He funded education and the arts. He loved the poetry of Robert Burns and could recite dozens of Shakespearean scenes from memory.

D.   Returning in glory to the land of his childhood, he bought Skibo Castle. The estate had 2,000 tenants and covered 32,000 acres of land.

E.   He led antiwar advocates in the early days of World War I.

Essential Reading:

Peter Krass, *Carnegie.*

Harold Livesay, *Andrew Carnegie and the Rise of Big Business.*

Supplementary Reading:

Andrew Carnegie, *Autobiography.*

Joseph Frazier Wall, *Andrew Carnegie.*

Questions to Consider:

1.   Did Carnegie do more good than harm, despite his ruthless methods?

2.   What prompted Carnegie to distribute his fortune as widely as possible, and how wisely did he carry out his plan?

Lecture Twenty-Three
"Buffalo Bill"—The Westerner

Scope: From the colonial period to the 1890s, there was always a western frontier for the European settlers of America. At first, it was just a few miles inland—Deerfield, Massachusetts, was a frontier town in 1700. By the late 18th century, it was the trans-Appalachian West, and the men who pioneered its settlement became heroes further East. Such men as Daniel Boone and Davy Crockett became western heroes in their own lifetimes and were legends by the time they died. William Cody, "Buffalo Bill," did the same thing on a larger scale a generation later. Singled out by eastern writers and editors as an ideal example of western manliness when he was only 23, he became the subject of hundreds of books, poems, plays, and exaggerated news stories. Realizing that others were capitalizing on his name and fame, Cody joined in. His riding show, Buffalo Bill's Wild West, helped create and enlarge the mythology of the American West during the last decades of the Plains Indian wars in the 1870s and 1880s. Several times, he had to leave off playing at Indian fighter to return to service as an actual Indian fighter; later, he staged fictionalized versions of his exploits, often using Indian survivors of the fighting as his hired actors. Images of the Wild West have long held a treasured place in Americans' conception of their own nation, and few people did more to nourish them than William Cody.

Outline

I. Raised on the Kansas Plains, Cody had a practical education in western outdoor life.

    A. Born in Iowa (1846), he moved with his family to the Kansas frontier in 1853.

    B. His father, a free-soil supporter and abolitionist, was killed by pro-slavery Kansans in 1855 at Fort Leavenworth.

    C. Poorly educated, Cody worked as a teamster and express rider.

        1. He worked as a cattle drover in a supply column in the anti-Mormon campaign of 1857.

2. He rode for the Pony Express, carrying mail from Sacramento, California to St. Joseph, Missouri.

D. He fought in irregular frontier campaigns of the Civil War before joining the Union Army.

    1. Bloody and ruthless fighting marked the Civil War in Kansas and Missouri between pro-Confederate Bushwhackers and pro-Union Jayhawkers.

    2. Cody served without distinction in a Kansas regiment of the Union army (despite later embroidered accounts of heroic wartime exploits).

II. Cody's genuine skills as a scout, soldier, and teamster led to his being singled out for mythological treatment.

A. His knowledge of the Kansas Plains country made him a useful army scout.

    1. General Philip Sheridan admired him for his knowledge of the terrain and his ability to ride long distances at high speed with messages.

    2. Between campaigns, he provided meat to railroad crews on the Kansas Pacific line.

    3. He grew his hair and mustache long and adopted fringed buckskin jackets.

B. Restlessness and an unsuitable marriage made Cody eager for adventure.

C. Journalist Ned Buntline singled him out for heroic literary treatment.

D. "Colonel" Prentiss Ingraham wrote 203 Buffalo Bill novels.

E. Eastern dignitaries and a Russian prince chose Cody as their guide to Plains buffalo hunting.

    1. He guided Yale professor Othniel Marsh in search of dinosaur fossils to the Big Horn Basin in 1870.

    2. He guided James Gordon Bennett of the *New York Herald*, Leonard Jerome, and other New York millionaires on a hunting expedition in 1871.

    3. Grand Duke Alexis, son of the czar, visited the Plains in early 1872, and Cody again guided him on a buffalo hunt.

    4. Bennett and other socialites hosted Cody on a successful visit to New York.

F. Recalled to the army from New York in 1873, Cody won the Congressional Medal of Honor in a campaign against the Sioux.

III. His exhibitions made him world famous and helped shape western mythology.

    A. Cody and Buntline staged "Scouts of the Plains" in 1872–1873.

        1. His drinking buddy "Wild Bill" Hickok proved an unsuitable addition to the troupe.

        2. A new promoter John Burke, nicknamed "Arizona John," improved the quality of the shows.

        3. Cody's participation in the 1876 campaign and the scalping of Yellow Hand became central elements in the Buffalo Bill myth.

    B. Cody thought of "The Wild West," which he founded in 1882, as educational rather than simply as entertainment and did not call it a "show."

        1. A series of tableaux showed the development of white civilization on the Plains.

        2. Between scenes, sharpshooters, such as Annie Oakley; stunt-riders; and calf-ropers, including Bill himself, astonished the crowd.

        3. Indians who had fought against settlers and the army often participated, including Sitting Bull.

    C. Buffalo Bill's Wild West toured American and European cities in 1886–1887 and later incorporated riders from Latin America, Russia, and Arabia.

        1. Moving it became a complex and sophisticated operation.

        2. It played next door to the 1893 Columbian Exhibition in Chicago.

    D. The figure of Buffalo Bill continued to dominate the mythological American West throughout the 20th century. Western movies followed many of the conventions established by his entertainments and by dime novels.

Essential Reading:

Robert A. Carter, *Buffalo Bill Cody: The Man Behind the Legend.*

R. L. Wilson, *Buffalo Bill's Wild West: An American Legend.*

Supplementary Reading:

Joy S. Kasson, *Buffalo Bill's Wild West: Celebrity: Memory, and Popular History.*

Richard Slotkin, *Gunfighter Nation: The Myth of the Frontier in the Twentieth Century.*

Questions to Consider:

1. What genuine qualities in William Cody enabled him to succeed as an idealized American westerner?

2. Are you convinced that the Wild West was educational rather than just an entertainment sensation?

Lecture Twenty-Four
Black Elk—The Holy Man

Scope: As we approach the halfway point of this course, it is in order to reemphasize a point made at the beginning. We should not think of the American identity as something static, a set of qualities that holds good throughout all of the nation's history. There may be some continuous threads and plenty of trends, but there are also immense changes—the disappearance of some obsessions and the development of new ones. We've witnessed the development of an intense faith in individualism, in democracy, in education, and in an active approach to problem solving, a general refusal to be fatalistic. Over these first two dozen lectures, we've also seen the way in which faith in science and progress were matched with faith in the idea of human equality, so that the great anomaly of slavery had to be destroyed. The story of Black Elk brings this second part of the series to a fitting close. He was a Plains Indian, an Oglala man of the Sioux or Lakota peoples. Born in 1863, he was present as a 13-year-old at the Battle of the Little Big Horn, witnessed what the army referred to as "Custer's Last Stand," and roamed the battlefield plundering the dead soldiers' bodies. Vouchsafed a powerful vision as a child, he believed it was his destiny to offer spiritual guidance to his people, but they were people undergoing even more rapid changes than those affecting all other Americans. By the time Black Elk was 30, the possibility of an independent life had ended for all American Indians, with profound consequences for their material, psychological, and spiritual lives. Wars between Indians and whites, and mutual fears, had been a continuous theme of American history for 300 years, but now ended.

Outline

I.   It is a common misconception to think of the Plains Indians' lives as unchanging before their direct encounter with settlers.

   A.   In reality, disease was transforming American Indian demography from the era of Columbus onwards. Whatever the exact population figures, it is true that disease drastically reduced Indian population and weakened peoples' ability to resist white incursions.

B. Population shifts predated direct contact for most Indian nations. Black Elk's people, the Latoka, or Sioux, were eastern woodland peoples originally and migrated onto the Plains, adapting there, under pressure from the East.

C. Horses, introduced by the Spanish conquistadors, transformed the Plains Indians' way of life before they met any white men.

II. Black Elk belonged to the last generation of Sioux that lived a semi-nomadic life on the Plains, dependent on buffalo hunting.

A. Born in 1863 near the Black Hills, his father and grandfather were both renowned shamans and healers.

B. At the age of 9, he received a powerful vision, which set the course of his life.

C. Like other Sioux boys, he learned to hunt buffalo and to fish.

D. As a 13-year-old, he witnessed the Battle of the Little Big Horn in 1876.

    1. He later described his battlefield experiences.

    2. After the battle, he and his family suffered a horrific winter pursuit by the army.

    3. He, like other survivors of the hard 1876–1877 winter, was obliged to settle on the Pine Ridge Reservation in South Dakota.

    4. After the assassination of Crazy Horse that summer, he joined a band that went to Canada rather than to another reservation.

E. A further vision intensified Black Elk's religious vocation in 1882.

F. In 1886, he joined Buffalo Bill's Wild West and traveled to Europe.

    1. He learned some English for the first time.

    2. He performed at Queen Victoria's Golden Jubilee celebrations in 1887.

G. Black Elk joined the millennial Ghost Dance cult.

    1. Ghost Dancers believed that they were invulnerable to bullets, that the white men would disappear, and that the buffalo would return.

2. Black Elk witnessed the Wounded Knee massacre of December 1890.

III. The events of his later life were less dramatic, but interpretation of their meaning has created an academic dispute.

    A. Most of what we know about Black Elk depends on writings from the 1930s and 1940s, based on his conversations with John Neihardt.

        1. Neihardt shaped *Black Elk Speaks* partly according to his own preoccupations.

        2. Black Elk's remarks condemn American selfishness and inequality in a way that might be a paraphrase of Neihardt.

        3. Neihardt also gave the misleading impression that Black Elk was about to die in 1931.

    B. Raymond DeMallie and other scholars subsequently drew a quite different picture, describing and explaining Black Elk's later life.

        1. He converted to Roman Catholicism at the Jesuit mission in 1904, at the age of 41.

        2. He devoted the later years of his life to intense Catholic proselytizing.

    C. He appears to have sought ways to unify old Sioux traditions and rituals with those of Catholic Christianity.

        1. This fact enables other scholars, such as Julian Rice, to doubt the whole-heartedness of Black Elk's Catholicism.

        2. Black Elk's legacy is academically and politically controversial.

Essential Reading:

Raymond DeMallie, *The Sixth Grandfather: Black Elk's Teachings Given to John G. Neihardt.*

John Neihardt, *Black Elk Speaks*.

Supplementary Reading:

William K. Powers, *Oglala Religion*.

Robert M. Utley, *The Last Days of the Sioux Nation*.

Questions to Consider:

1. Is it surprising or predictable that Black Elk should have become a Christian in later life?

2. Is there any way of avoiding uncertainty in the analysis and interpretation of historical records, especially oral records?

Lecture Twenty-Five
John Wesley Powell—The Desert Theorist

Scope: Buffalo Bill and Black Elk both witnessed the rapid transformation of the Great Plains West from a land of nomadic buffalo hunters to a land of settled homestead farmers and ranchers. The land even further west, the mountains and deserts, presented even harsher challenges to American settlers than the largely treeless plains. The man whose adventures, ideas, and analysis left the deepest impression on this region was John Wesley Powell (1834–1902). Personally fearless, he was the first man to travel the length of the Grand Canyon in a boat. Intellectually adventurous, he learned the languages of the desert Indians and became a leading ethnographer and anthropologist. At the same time, he did vital work mapping the terrain and geology of the desert southwest. As a politician at the U.S. Geological Survey, finally, Powell proposed a dramatic and novel solution to the chronic western problem of water shortage. Just as any study of American parkland has to begin with Frederick Law Olmsted, so any study of the desert southwest has to begin with John Wesley Powell.

Outline

I.   The son of a Methodist preacher and abolitionist, Powell became fascinated by science as a child.

   A. Stoned by other children because of his father's abolitionist militancy, he studied with a local scientist, George Crookham, in Jackson, Ohio.

      1. The family moved to a Wisconsin farm in 1846, later to Illinois, and finally, to Kansas.

      2. Powell paid his way through colleges in Illinois by working as a teacher.

   B. A Union army officer on General Grant's staff, he was wounded at the Battle of Shiloh, and his right forearm was amputated.

   C. He remained in the service and fought with distinction as an artillery officer until 1865, rising to the brevet rank of lieutenant colonel.

D. He became a college professor of geology at Illinois Wesleyan University in Bloomington and organized fossil collections for the state university's museum.

II. Powell explored the Grand Canyon by boat and the surrounding lands on horseback in 1869 and the 1870s.

    A. His first downriver expedition began in 1869, the year when the first transcontinental railroad could take his boats and crew to Green River, Wyoming.

        1. They followed Green River to its confluence with the Grand, then through the canyon itself, a 99-day journey.

        2. Severe hardships and near-starvation led three members of the expedition to abandon the attempt.

        3. Ironically, those who stayed with Powell were the ones who survived.

    B. A second boat expedition in 1871–1872 permitted further observation and mapping and was accompanied by a surveyor and photographer.

        1. Powell's book *The Exploration of the Colorado*, a mixture of science and high adventure, was published in 1875, eliding elements of the two expeditions.

        2. His *Geographical and Geological Survey of the Rocky Mountain Region* won army and government patronage and support from the Smithsonian.

III. Political and publicity skills enabled Powell to play a significant role in the economic and political development of the area.

    A. Powell's *Report on the Arid Regions* (1878) argued for a completely new approach to land use in the desert west.

        1. The surveyed grid of 640-acre square miles had worked well in the humid zones, where a quarter section of 160 acres made a viable homestead farm, depending on rainfall.

        2. Powell argued that most desert land was unfarmable, except with irrigation and new forms of organization.

        3. At first, Congress rejected what it saw as Powell's excessively pessimistic approach to western settlement.

        4. The Newlands Act of 1902, however, embodied much of Powell's wisdom.

B. Powell won two major appointments, as director of the Bureau of Indian Ethnology from 1879 until his death in 1902 and as director of the U.S. Geological Survey (1881–1894).

    1. He befriended Ute, Shivwitz, Paiute, Hopi, Shoshone and other southwestern Indians on all his expeditions and became expert in their languages and cultures.

    2. He attempted to apply evolutionary theory to the stages of Indian culture and to systematize American knowledge of the native peoples.

Essential Reading:

John Wesley Powell, *The Exploration of the Colorado River and Its Canyons.*

Wallace Stegner, *Beyond the Hundredth Meridian: John Wesley Powell and the Second Opening of the West.*

Supplementary Reading:

Marc Reisner, *Cadillac Desert: The American West and Its Disappearing Water.*

Donald Worster, *A River Running West: The Life of John Wesley Powell.*

Questions to Consider:

1. How did Powell's frontier and wartime experiences contribute to his scientific and political career?

2. Why, according to Powell, did the political and economic organization of the West have to be completely different from that of the lands east of the Mississippi?

Lecture Twenty-Six
William Mulholland—The Water Engineer

Scope: William Mulholland's career takes up where John Wesley Powell's left off, though he has a less honorable place in American history. He was the man who made it possible for cities to grow in the desert country of the American southwest. Phoenix, Las Vegas, and above all, Los Angeles could never have become major cities except for his insight that scarce water resources, essential if a city's growth were to continue, could be carried over long distances by aqueduct. Mulholland (1855–1935) was an Irish immigrant who traveled throughout the West before joining the Los Angeles Water Department. Working equally for the city and for himself, he exploited first the local aquifers, then the Owens River Valley, diverting almost the entire flow of its river into an aqueduct that ran across 200 miles of desert. The farmers of Owens Valley, stripped of an asset without which their land would be worthless, retaliated in 1924 by dynamiting the aqueduct and setting off the Owens Valley War, which drew worldwide press notice. Mulholland's reputation, tainted in the affair, was ruined in 1928 when the St. Francis Dam, whose building he had authorized and supervised, burst, creating a catastrophic tidal wave and killing 500 people. His legacy, of massive water-diversion projects, remains controversial, particularly because of their environmental effects and their concentration of power in the hands of a small wealthy elite.

Outline

I. Mulholland, an Irish immigrant, traveled widely before coming to Los Angeles in 1878.

A. He was born in Ireland and raised there, in Dublin, up to age 15.

1. He ran away to sea in 1870, settling in America four years later.

2. He worked as a lumberman in the Michigan forests and as a dry-goods salesman in Pittsburgh.

3. He first experienced the water-starved southwest as a miner and Indian fighter in Arizona.

4. He arrived in Los Angeles in 1878, when it had a population under 10,000.

B. Mulholland's first job for the private Los Angeles Water Company was as a ditch cleaner.

II. When Los Angeles took over the water system, it hired Mulholland as head of the Department of Water and Power, a job he retained until 1928.

A. He first developed local aquifers but foresaw that they would soon be exhausted. Aware of the depletion, he began conserving rainfall water, channeling it into the aquifer and reducing runoff.

B. Collaborating with former mayor Fred Eaton to ensure the city's continued growth, Mulholland planned to divert the Owens River, more than 200 miles distant.

1. Flowing out of the Sierra Nevada Mountains, the river served as the water supply of an irrigation-farming project.

2. Eaton and Mulholland bought lands beside the Owens River from which their diversion was to be made.

C. Mulholland notified a consortium of businessmen that they would be able to enrich themselves by buying land in the San Fernando Valley. They then helped pass the bond issue that financed the diversion of the Owens River in 1905, while Congress gave the aqueduct rights-of-way across the public domain in 1906.

D. Between 1905 and 1913, the Los Angeles Aqueduct was designed and built.

1. It carried Owens River waters more than 230 miles across desert and mountains.

2. It required elaborate engineering, including a railroad line, roads, power lines, and 164 tunnels.

3. At its completion, however, it gave Los Angeles more water than the city needed, so that San Fernando farmers were the main beneficiaries.

E. Angry citizens of the Owens Valley, whose own livelihood had been damaged by the aqueduct, dynamited a section of it in 1924.

1. Alleging that Mulholland was in the hands of a sinister Jewish cabal, many of these citizens were Ku Klux Klan members.

2. In November 1924, they diverted the river flow completely, winning widespread public sympathy.

3. Armed guards patrolled the aqueduct but could not prevent another bombing in 1927.

F. The bankruptcy of his principal Owens Valley rivals in 1927 seemed to guarantee victory for Mulholland.

III. Mulholland, appearing to have defeated Owens Valley, was ruined when he was implicated in the collapse of the defective St. Francis Dam in 1928.

A. Imperfectly constructed, the dam's failure released 15 billion gallons of water into the Santa Clara Valley, north of Los Angeles.

1. It created a tidal wave 75 feet high.

2. As it rushed 54 miles to the sea, it killed about 500 people and devastated large areas of Ventura County.

B. An investigation blamed Mulholland for ignoring danger signs and filling the dam too quickly.

1. It showed that the dam had been poorly sited and that its foundations were unsound.

2. Mulholland accepted responsibility, saying, "If there is an error of human judgment, I am the human."

C. He resigned in disgrace and died in 1935.

D. Historians continue to dispute his culpability, with his granddaughter Catherine Mulholland leading the charge to exonerate his name.

IV. Immense water projects continued to transform the southwest and to facilitate urbanization in the area, which had previously seemed too dry for all but modest settlements. They are Mulholland's legacy, for good and ill.

A. The Bureau of Reclamation (founded by the Newlands Act of 1902) and the Army Corps of Engineers completed four massive dam-building jobs.

B. Theoretically, the Bureau of Reclamation supported small-scale irrigation farmers, but in reality, it was a bonanza for corporate agribusiness.

C. The Hoover Dam exploited some of the potential of the Colorado River.

1. It provided work to thousands of Depression-era workmen.

    2. It stored more than a year's supply of river water and controlled the flow downstream.

D. Further exploitation of the Colorado was eventually restrained by environmentalists' criticism. When Floyd Dominy of the Bureau of Reclamation planned a reservoir in the Grand Canyon, David Brower and the Sierra Club fought back successfully.

E. The sustainability of western cities remains controversial.

Essential Reading:

Margaret Leslie Davis, *Rivers in the Desert: William Mulholland and the Inventing of Los Angeles.*

Catherine Mulholland, *William Mulholland and the Rise of Los Angeles.*

Supplementary Reading:

Norris Hundley, *The Great Thirst: Californians and Water.*

Marc Reisner, *Cadillac Desert: The American West and Its Disappearing Water.*

Questions to Consider:

1. What combination of personal ambitions and real urban needs in Los Angeles combined to make the aqueduct possible?

2. What were Mulholland's greatest strengths and weaknesses as an engineer and politician?

Lecture Twenty-Seven
Samuel Gompers—The Trade Unionist

Scope: The history of the West in the late 19th century is a vast and colorful story, which generated such vivid characters as Buffalo Bill and John Wesley Powell. But for every American or immigrant who tried his luck in the West, 50 more stayed east of the Mississippi and swelled the rapidly growing industrial cities, working for the great new entrepreneurs, including Andrew Carnegie. The decades between 1860 and 1920 witnessed the transformation of America from a predominantly rural to a predominantly urban society; by the latter date, most Americans lived in towns and cities and only a minority made their living from farming. These were also the active years of Samuel Gompers's life. Born in 1850, he emigrated from Britain to America in 1863 and devoted his whole adult life to the trade union cause. Aware that the great industrialists regarded labor simply as one of their costs, he embodied workers' demand that their dignity as independent citizens be preserved, that they be paid decent wages, work in safe conditions, and enjoy job security. A founder and first president of the American Federation of Labor, Gompers became a heroic figure to millions of American workingmen. Moreover, as trade unionism gradually became an established element of the industrial order, entrepreneurs and politicians began to honor the socially conservative Gompers, especially when the alternatives appeared to be socialists, such as Eugene Debs, or anarchists, such as Emma Goldman and Big Bill Haywood.

Outline

I. Raised in London by working-class Jews, Gompers began life as a child laborer.

    A. His parents, recent immigrants from Holland, sent him to work in the shoe business after a few years at the London Jewish Free School.

    B. He switched to cigar-making, the trade in which his father worked and was active as a trade unionist.

C. The family migrated to New York in 1863 in search of better opportunities and stayed in the same trade.

    1. Cigar-makers had a reputation for learning and disputation.

    2. Mechanization of the trade in 1868 opened it to unskilled workers and brought the old workshop craft to an end.

II. Gompers rose to leadership in the Cigar Makers' Union, Local 144, and gradually learned of the need for organization across cities and trades.

    A. He belonged to a group of idealistic unionists who named themselves *Die Zehn Philosophen*, or "the Ten Philosophers."

        1. He argued that unions must try to incorporate unskilled, as well as skilled laborers.

        2. He argued that workers should concentrate on workplace issues and not let themselves be distracted by politics.

    B. Gompers was a delegate in 1881 to the Federation of Organized Trades and Labor Unions.

    C. He challenged the Knights of Labor for its utopian approach to unionism.

    D. The Federation was reorganized in 1886 as the American Federation of Labor (AFL), with Gompers as its first president.

        1. AFL unions were, in practice, generally those of skilled workmen, who could be less easily displaced by strikebreakers than the unskilled.

        2. Under Gompers's pragmatic leadership, the AFL avoided political radicalism and simply tried to ensure improved pay and conditions for its members.

        3. The AFL accepted the characteristic voluntarism of the American system and rarely sought political solutions for economic conflicts.

        4. Gompers and most AFL unions' members shared the social prejudices of their era, favoring Chinese exclusion and remaining lukewarm about African-Americans' rights.

        5. Anarchists and socialists criticized Gompers's apparent acquiescence in the socioeconomic status quo, and he attacked them for violating the American tradition.

III. In the corporate era of the early 20th century, Gompers became the most frequent representative of labor on nationwide political and progressive committees.

    A. The AFL's British counterpart, the TUC, created a Labour Party at the beginning of the 20th century, leading to a dramatic contrast in national experiences.

    B. Gompers became a founding member and vice president of the National Civic Federation (NCF), cooperating with leading businessmen and politicians, even those who opposed unions in their own factories.

        1. Unions still lacked even a guarantee of legality.

        2. NCF members favored welfare capitalism and were less hostile to the AFL than members of the National Association of Manufacturers.

    C. The AFL moderated its nonpartisan stance in the second decade of the 20th century and benefited from supporters in the Wilson administration.

        1. Pro-labor legislation in Wilson's first administration led Gompers to campaign vigorously for Wilson's reelection in 1916.

        2. Gompers worked for Wilson's preparedness campaign and was an outspoken anti-socialist during World War I.

        3. The AFL's participation in the National War Labor Board was an indication that it had become a recognized, permanent part of the political nation.

        4. Wilson's death and an era of Republican ascendancy in the 1920s led to a widespread assault by industry on trade unions.

    D. Gompers died in 1924 in San Antonio after attending a Mexican meeting of the Pan-American Federation of Labor.

    E. He imparted to American trade unionism a non-radical legacy and a smaller role in national political life than British, French, and German unions played.

Essential Reading:

Samuel Gompers, *Seventy Years of Life and Labor*, Nick Salvatore, ed.

Julie Greene, *Pure and Simple Politics: The American Federation of Labor and Political Activism*.

Harold Livesay, *Samuel Gompers and Organized Labor in America.*

Supplementary Reading:

Stuart B. Kaufman, *Samuel Gompers and the Origins of the American Federation of Labor.*

Questions to Consider:

1. What qualities made Gompers so effective as a labor leader for so long?

2. Was his opposition to other immigrants coherent and justifiable?

Lecture Twenty-Eight
Booker T. Washington—The "Race Leader"

Scope: Booker T. Washington was born a slave, but as an educator and "race-leader," he rose to a position of wealth and influence. His is one of the greatest examples in American history of the rise from rags to riches—in the last 20 years of his life, he was the most powerful and politically influential African-American in the country. He was widely criticized in his own day, however, and his historical reputation is ambiguous. At a time when racial segregation was worsening, when African-Americans were losing the right to vote, and when an epidemic of lynching spread across the South, jeopardizing the lives and safety of African-Americans, Washington advocated racial conciliation and cooperation and rarely spoke out against injustice. His rival, W. E. B. DuBois, was passionately outspoken against these outrages and became one of Washington's most pungent and public critics. Even when Washington worked against segregation and disfranchisement, he did it secretly, behind the scenes, and publicly disclaimed any interest in politics.

Outline

I. Early experiences convinced Washington that he must become educated.

   A. Born on a Virginia tobacco farm, he was a slave for the first nine years of his life.

   B. After emancipation, his family moved to Malden, West Virginia, to work at the salt mines and furnaces.

   C. His early schooling took place at night, after work.

   D. Working for Mrs. Viola Ruffner as a house servant taught him the Victorian values of punctuality, sobriety, orderliness, and cleanliness.

   E. Washington walked 500 miles to Hampton, Virginia, to enroll in Samuel Armstrong's industrial school, where he worked his way through college.

1. The methods and expectations of the school transformed him and made a deep, permanent impression on his approach to life.

   2. After graduation, Washington briefly considered teaching and law as professions.

   3. Armstrong recalled him to be a Hampton teacher in 1879.

II. Washington took over the new Tuskegee Institute and made it America's premier agricultural and industrial school for black students.

   A. Students built the school, then ran it.

   B. Washington, a superb orator, went on extensive fundraising tours to the North and proved a skillful fundraiser. He also secured the help of sympathetic southern whites.

   C. He won the support of Carnegie, Rockefeller, and other businessman/philanthropists.

   D. He argued that learning basic industrial and agricultural skills was more important than abstract intellectual work.

   E. In practice, most graduates became teachers.

   F. Washington became a board member at other black colleges and aided their fundraising drives.

III. Washington became a national African-American leader in 1895 and wielded political influence but gained political opponents.

   A. His speech at the Cotton States Exposition in 1895 made him nationally famous as an advocate of racial conciliation and cooperation.

   1. He claimed that there was a perfect harmony of interests between black and white southerners.

   2. President Cleveland sent him a letter of congratulation.

   3. He never supported segregation, but he urged black Americans, at least for the moment, to live with it.

   4. His autobiography, *Up from Slavery* (1901), quickly became an inspirational classic.

   B. President Theodore Roosevelt singled Washington out as a leader, and the two cooperated.

   1. Washington dined at the White House in 1901.

   2. Roosevelt sought Washington's advice on appointments.

   3. In return, Washington delivered the black vote.

4. An international celebrity, he also dined with Queen Victoria.

C. Washington worked behind the scenes against segregation, lynching, and disfranchisement but only rarely made public statements against them.

D. Washington's most formidable critic was W. E. B. DuBois, who helped create the National Association for the Advancement of Colored People.

Essential Reading:

Louis Harlan, *Booker T. Washington: The Wizard of Tuskegee.*

Booker T. Washington, *Up from Slavery.*

Supplementary Reading:

Jacqueline M. Moore, *Booker T. Washington, W. E. B. DuBois and the Struggle for Racial Uplift.*

John White, *Black Leadership in America: From Booker T. Washington to Jesse Jackson.*

Questions to Consider:

1. Was Washington reasonable in accepting segregation, in view of prevailing conditions of the 1890s and 1900s?

2. What qualities in Washington made him able to achieve so much in the face of so many obstacles?

Lecture Twenty-Nine
Emma Goldman—The Anarchist

Scope: In the last two lectures, we have witnessed leaders who valued compromise—Gompers compromised with the capitalist moguls, and Washington compromised with the segregationists. Both of them enjoyed power and authority but suffered accusations of having sold out the people they should have led. Emma Goldman (1869–1940), by contrast, specialized in not compromising and, in consequence, could never be a leader. One of the two or three best known anarchists in American history, she was widely feared and hated in her own lifetime but has become, retrospectively, one of the nation's most popular women. She believed that government of any kind was repressive and that the use of force to overthrow it would be justified. She participated in a plot to assassinate Henry Clay Frick, an industrialist, and she was one of the most ardent American supporters of the Russian Revolution when it began in 1917. She had countless other qualities to make her abhorrent to her contemporaries; she believed in free love, birth control, abortion, and women's rights. Goldman was a Jewish immigrant like Samuel Gompers, but the path of his lifetime was toward respectability and mainstream values. Hers was, if anything, away from respectability, and she finally enraged the authorities to such a degree that she was first imprisoned, then deported, for her radical views and actions.

Outline

I. Born and raised in the Russian empire, Goldman emigrated to America in 1885 and became involved in working-class radical politics.

    A. She came from a family of declining middle-class Jews in Kovno, Lithuania.

    B. An emigrant to Rochester, New York, at the age of 16, Goldman worked in a clothing factory and made a disastrous early marriage.

    C. The Haymarket bombing and trials awakened her to working-class politics.

II. Learning her anarchism from Johann Most and Alexander Berkmann, she became more famous than either as a representative of the cause.

   A. She conspired with Berkmann to assassinate Henry Clay Frick after the Homestead strike and confrontation in 1892.

      1. They were so poor that they could not afford two train tickets to Pittsburgh, so Berkmann went alone.

      2. He shot and stabbed Frick, who nevertheless recovered, and Berkmann paid for his act with 14 years in prison.

   B. Goldman began to lecture throughout the United States on anarchism. She spent a year in prison (1893–1894) for speeches arguing that the hungry unemployed had a right to steal food.

   C. During a visit to Austria, she studied nursing and frequently put that training to use in later years.

   D. She defended Leon Czolgosz, the man who assassinated President McKinley.

III. Goldman's ideas about women's position in society were as unconventional as her political views.

   A. She was sexually aggressive at a time when women were expected to be reticent.

      1. Having already taken lovers in Russia, she was dismayed to find her first husband impotent.

      2. She also loved dancing and smoking, was a good cook, and took pleasure in all sensual activities.

   B. She believed in free love but found it difficult not to be possessive in practice.

   C. Goldman helped women who needed birth control or access to abortion at a time when both were illegal.

IV. Goldman was a distinguished public speaker and writer, not only on anarchism but on politics and literature.

   A. Strindberg and Ibsen were among the subjects on which she lectured.

      1. She published *Anarchism and Other Essays* (1910) and *The Social Significance of the Modern Drama* (1914).

      2. Her journal *Mother Earth* debated art and politics between 1906 and 1917.

B. Younger radicals found her a persuasive advocate of anarchism.

V. Opposition to America's role in World War I, followed by support for the Russian Revolution, led first to imprisonment for Goldman and Berkmann, then to deportation.

    A. Goldman was convicted in 1917 for interfering with the military draft and served a two-year prison term in Jefferson City, Missouri.

    B. Deported in 1919 with 250 foreign-born radicals, she began as an eager supporter of Lenin and Trotsky.

    C. She believed the Soviet Union could eliminate all social injustice and repression.

    D. Soviet repression, culminating with its suppression of the Kronstadt sailors, disillusioned Goldman to the degree that she and Berkmann abandoned the Soviet Union.

    E. In exile, she became a leading left-wing anticommunist and authored *My Disillusionment with Russia* (1923).

    F. She lived the later years of her life in England, France, and Canada.

    G. Publication of her memoirs, *Living My Life* (1931), enhanced Goldman's worldwide literary reputation and led to her only post-1919 visit to the United States.

    H. Visiting Spain regularly during its Civil War (1936–1939), she propagandized on behalf of the anarchist forces on the republican side.

Essential Reading:

Martin Duberman, *Mother Earth: An Epic Drama of Emma Goldman's Life*.

Emma Goldman, *Living My Life*, 2 vols.

Supplementary Reading:

Candace Falk, *Love, Anarchy, and Emma Goldman*.

Marian Morton, *Emma Goldman and the American Left: Nowhere at Home*.

Questions to Consider:

1. Why was anarchism so attractive to Goldman and so horrifying to most of her American contemporaries?

2. Is Goldman a suitable role model for contemporary feminists?

Lecture Thirty
Abraham Cahan—The Immigrants' Advocate

Scope: In the late 19th and early 20th centuries, millions of Southern and Eastern Europeans emigrated to America in search of economic opportunity and to escape tyranny and intolerance at home. Emma Goldman was among them, but she rejected the American ideal of success. Abraham Cahan (1860–1951) was among them, too, and he, after a long flirtation with socialism, eventually accepted it. Arriving in New York at age 22, Cahan eventually founded a Yiddish-language newspaper for his fellow Jewish immigrants, the *Jewish Daily Forward*, and used it to tutor them in adapting to America's alien way of life. His advice column, the "Bintel Brief," was one of the first of its kind, and it offered practical advice to ordinary immigrants about how to handle the problems of their everyday lives. A distinguished novelist in English and Yiddish, Cahan won the respect of prominent figures in the American literary world, above all, for his semi-autobiographical novel, *The Rise of David Levinsky* (1917).

Outline

I. Anti-Jewish pogroms after 1880 prompted a large-scale Jewish migration from Eastern Europe, much of which found its way to the Lower East Side of New York.

   A. Cahan fled from his Lithuanian home under threat of arrest and joined an emigrant train across Europe.

   B. He traveled through the Austro-Hungarian Empire and Germany, to England, and thence, to the United States, arriving in 1882.

   C. Cahan's talent for languages ensured that he would not be confined to monotonous factory work for long.

   1. He had begun learning English on the ship with the help of a sympathetic steerage steward.

   2. After a few weeks in workshops, he began tutoring other immigrants in English.

   3. He became a public school teacher after sitting in on much younger students' classes to improve his own English.

D. An idealistic socialist, Cahan spoke on the subject in Yiddish, Russian, and English during the 1880s and early 1890s.

  1. Most of the early Jewish radicals preferred Russian, but Cahan convinced them that they would have to use Yiddish to attract more recruits.

  2. Cahan was thrilled by his ability to rouse audiences and by the fact that, in America, he really could exercise freedom of speech.

  3. He was not very learned in socialist theory and vacillated between rival forms of radicalism in his early American years.

  4. In 1893, he was an American delegate to the Brussels and Vienna conferences of the Second International (a conference of the worldwide movement of socialists who hoped to bring about revolution peacefully) but was shocked to discover the anti-Semitism of many European socialists.

  5. Later, in 1917, he was excited at first by the outbreak of the Russian Revolution but soon became disenchanted by the Red terror and mass rural starvation.

II. Cahan's talent as a writer in English of stories about immigrant life drew the notice of influential American critics and helped create his role as an interpreter between the older Anglo population and the Jewish immigrants.

  A. William Dean Howells, the most influential critic of his day, praised Cahan's first English story, "A Providential Match."

  1. It exhibited the same kind of realism that Howells had developed in his own *Rise of Silas Lapham*.

  2. Cahan's first English novel, *Yekl: A Tale of the New York Ghetto* (1896), also won critical acclaim.

  B. Lincoln Steffens invited Cahan to join the staff of the *New York Commercial Advertiser*.

  1. The 1890s and 1900s was an age of great dynamism among American newspapers, under the direction of such owners as Pulitzer and Hearst and undistracted by the competition of radio and television.

  2. Cahan's stories explained intergenerational tensions in immigrant families.

III. The *Jewish Daily Forward* was the paper he edited almost continually from 1903 to his death in 1951.

A. The paper was founded in 1897 as a general Yiddish newspaper for immigrants. Cahan was its first editor but resigned twice in the early years because of editorial disagreements with his board.

B. The "Bintel Brief" (bundle of letters) was an early "agony column," which today gives us a vivid glimpse into the trials and tribulations of early Jewish settlers in New York.

1. One set of problems dealt with how marriages should be arranged.
2. Other problems included crowded living conditions in tenement buildings and hard-hearted employers.
3. "Bintel Briefs" often investigated how to practice traditional Judaism in jarring new surroundings.

C. Cahan's editorial work, along with his own life experience, provided him with the rich material of his greatest novel, *The Rise of David Levinsky* (1917).

1. Its hero, in Europe, longs for a life of Talmudic study but is tempted by business opportunities when he arrives in America.
2. He becomes a success in the clothing trade, not least through sharp practice and deceit.
3. He loves America, yet looks back nostalgically on the way of life he has forsaken.

IV. Cahan was among the first in a distinguished lineage of American Jewish writers, first in Yiddish, then in English, who became central figures in the American literature of the mid- and late 20th century.

A. Successors refined the topics he had first introduced into American literature: Saul Bellow, Philip Roth, and Chaim Potok are outstanding examples in fiction writing.

B. Later Jewish journalism also owed a debt to Cahan; Norman Mailer's *new journalism* of the 1960s and 1970s emulated the emotional involvement and intensity Cahan had shown 60 years earlier.

Essential Reading:

Abraham Cahan, *The Rise of David Levinsky*.

Irving Howe, *World of Our Fathers: The Journey of the East European Jews to America and the Life They Found and Made*.

Supplementary Reading:

Stanford E. Marovitz, *Abraham Cahan.*

Moses Rischin, ed., *Grandma Never Lived in America: The New Journalism of Abraham Cahan.*

Questions to Consider:

1. What qualities did Cahan combine to make him such an effective advocate for, and observer of, immigrant Jewish life in America?

2. Was the assimilation of each new generation of immigrants to America inevitable?

Lecture Thirty-One
Isabella Stewart Gardner—The Collector

Scope: From the colonial period to the late 19th century, America had an undistinguished artistic heritage; many of the nation's talented painters and sculptors emigrated to Europe. Not until the 1950s would New York become an important international center of the arts. In the late 19th century, however, a group of extraordinarily wealthy Americans began collecting art and cultural artifacts from Europe, particularly Italy, building themselves lavish palaces in which to hoard their treasures. Many of the great American art collections were established then. None carries a more distinctive stamp than the Isabella Stewart Gardner Museum in Boston, a pseudo-Renaissance palace built in the first years of the 20th century by a wealthy widow. Friend and admirer of all the major Boston intellectuals and artists of her day and patron of the era's most famous connoisseur, Bernard Berenson, Gardner (1840–1923) showed a lifelong capacity for intellectual growth and development, becoming a major collector only in her 50s and creating the museum that immortalized her in her 60s and 70s.

Outline

I. Born to wealthy New York parents, Isabella Stewart Gardner enjoyed every financial and educational advantage of her era.

    A. She was born in 1840, the oldest of four siblings, to a Scottish-American father and a mother whose ancestors had been in America since the 1600s.

    B. Her father was a textile importer, distantly related to the Stuart monarchs of England and Scotland.

    C. She was educated by tutors and at a Paris finishing school.

    D. She married Jack Gardner, brother of one of her school friends, in 1860 and settled in Boston.

        1. The family's merchant business with China and, later, its railroad and manufacturing investments had made it extremely wealthy.

2. The death of Gardner's son, a miscarriage, and her inability to have more children induced a period of profound depression in the mid-1860s.

3. Jack Gardner revived her spirits by taking her on ambitious journeys to the Arctic, Egypt, Palestine, and throughout Europe.

E. The Gardners' Back Bay home became a leading intellectual and artistic salon in the1870s and 1880s.

F. Isabella's unconventional acts, such as borrowing a railroad locomotive and borrowing lion cubs from the zoo, made her a press favorite.

G. Unable to have children after 1865, she later adopted the three sons of her husband's deceased brother (a suicide) and raised them as her own.

H. In the early 1880s, she met and became passionately infatuated with the young novelist Francis Marion Crawford.

I. Her friendship with John Singer Sargent also gave rise to a controversial portrait, *Woman—An Enigma* (1888).

II. The Gardners began to buy paintings and statues, stained glass, books and manuscripts, and had built up a major collection from around the world by the 1890s.

A. They visited Japan, Cambodia, and Java in 1883 and began to spend long periods at a villa in Venice.

B. Bernard Berenson, the connoisseur, became Isabella's most important friend.

1. He was able to travel to Italy in the first place because of a financial gift from Isabella.

2. Berenson became her most important advisor, recommending works for her to pursue, checking against forgery, and negotiating with art dealers.

C. In the 1880s, she collected numerous paintings by the best French artists of the era, including Corot and Courbet, and by the Americans Sargent, LaFarge, and Whistler.

D. The Gardners' acquisition of paintings by Vermeer, Raphael, Botticelli, and Rubens in the 1890s marked them as major collectors.

III. Jack Gardner's sudden death in 1898 prompted Isabella's resolve to build a museum for their immense collection.

   A. She bought land in the Fenway area of Boston, a reclaimed swamp designed by Frederick Law Olmsted.

   B. She designed Fenway Court and closely supervised the builders.

      1. She insisted that it be built of the same materials and in the same manner as a Renaissance palace, refusing to incorporate steel or concrete into the structure.

      2. She often changed her mind and twice ordered the builders to dismantle staircases after they had been finished.

      3. Hundreds of pillars, columns, arches, staircases, and carved stone animals, all imported from Europe, were incorporated into the structure.

   C. Fenway Court, laid out according to Isabella's taste, opened to the public in 1903 and has remained almost unchanged ever since.

      1. In the early years, its collection was superior even to that of the Boston Museum of Fine Arts, situated nearby, which made Isabella a member of its acquisitions committee.

      2. The fourth floor of Fenway Court was Isabella's home—the first three housed the collection.

   D. Gardner died in 1924, specifying in her will that the collection as she had displayed it must remain exactly the same thenceforward.

      1. It is an important piece of American Edwardiana.

      2. Curators and benefactors are eager to modify it in some particulars.

IV. Other super-rich Americans of Gardner's era also became art collectors and palace builders.

   A. The millionaires' palaces at Newport, Rhode Island, were built to the same lavish scale as Fenway Court.

   B. The collections of Henry Clay Frick, Solomon Guggenheim, Henry Huntington, and later Paul Getty, eventually rivaled and surpassed Gardner's.

   C. Only after World War II did American art become world renowned, through the work of the Abstract Expressionists and the Pop Art movement.

   D. Gardner had patronized Cezanne, Derain, and Matisse but never enthused over the abstract works of the early modern artists.

Essential Reading:

Morris Carter, *Isabella Stewart Gardner and Fenway Court.*

Douglas Shand-Tucci, *The Art of Scandal: The Life and Times of Isabella Stewart Gardner.*

Supplementary Reading:

Hillard T. Goldfarb, *The Isabella Stewart Gardner Museum.*

Rollin Van Hadley, ed., *The Letters of Isabella Stewart Gardner and Bernard Berenson.*

Questions to Consider:

1. Why were so many of America's super-rich drawn to the idea of art collecting?

2. How did Isabella Stewart Gardner use her celebrity status?

Lecture Thirty-Two
Oliver Wendell Holmes—The Jurist

Scope: The Supreme Court has played a vital and continuous role in the history of the United States right from the beginning. Some of its decisions have become notorious, such as *Dred Scott v. Sanford* (1857), which denied elementary legal rights to slaves, and *Plessy v. Ferguson* (1896), which upheld racial segregation. Many more have been deeply controversial, winning enthusiastic support from some Americans and equally sharp condemnation from others— *Roe v. Wade* (1973) is a case in point. One of the most profound traits in the American identity is faith in the law, a faith that runs deep and ensures that the Supreme Court's decisions really matter. The judiciary is the least democratic branch of the government, by design, because the founders wanted to be sure that the justices would not be swayed by short-term political factors in deciding the law. Historians have always been fascinated by the men (and, more recently, women) chosen to serve on the nation's highest court. Some have been nonentities and some partisan, but a few have been individuals of immense erudition, whose life histories are remarkable in their own right. Few or none were greater than Oliver Wendell Holmes. Joining the court at the age of 61 in 1902, after a long and distinguished career as a legal theorist and in State Supreme Court, he served until 1932, aged 91. His life spans a vast era of American history. As a child, he knew Abigail Adams's son John Quincy, born in 1761; by the time he died, Ronald Reagan, who would be president in the 1980s, was starting his movie career.

Outline

I. Son of a doctor and writer, Oliver Wendell Holmes took advantage of a privileged childhood in Boston.

    A. Holmes enjoyed a first-class formal education and read widely.

        1. Raised in a learned and literary family, he attended the Dixwell Private Latin School to prepare for Harvard entrance.

        2. Entering Harvard at age 16, he graduated in 1861 as the Civil War began.

B. Immediately after graduating college, Holmes joined the Twentieth Massachusetts Infantry at the start of the Civil War and was commissioned as a lieutenant.

    1. He was wounded in three battles, Ball's Bluff, Antietam, and Fredericksburg.

    2. He reached the brevet rank of lieutenant colonel (the same as John Wesley Powell) before leaving the service in 1864.

II. Holmes embarked on a legal career of almost unequaled distinction.

    A. He graduated from Harvard Law School in 1866 and passed the Massachusetts bar the following year.

    B. He joined many of the most eminent New Englanders of his day in the Metaphysical Club.

    C. He was skilled as an author and editor.

        1. He became editor of the *American Law Review* in 1870.

        2. He edited the 12th edition of Kent's *Commentaries* (1873).

        3. *The Common Law* (1881) was based on a series of his lectures on the foundations of American law.

    D. Holmes became a professor at Harvard Law School in 1882 but resigned after one semester to become a member of the Massachusetts Supreme Judicial Court.

    E. For 20 years, he dominated the court, becoming its chief justice in 1899.

    F. His decisions and dissents showed the theoretical insights of *The Common Law* at work in practice.

III. President Theodore Roosevelt nominated Holmes to the U.S. Supreme Court in 1902, and he served for more than 30 years, becoming famous as a dissenter.

    A. He dismayed Roosevelt by writing a dissent in the important *Northern Securities Case* (1905), which represented the president's great challenge to corporate power.

    B. On labor issues, Holmes argued that the court ought to guard itself against subscribing to a particular economic theory, *laissez faire*, and that it should be willing to accept the development of trade unions and their members' right to strike.

1. In *Lochner v. New York* (1905) and *Muller v. Oregon* (1909), Holmes accepted the right of the state to specify hours and working conditions.
2. He admired, and later became a close ally of, Louis Brandeis, who first used sociological evidence before the court in *Muller*.

C. Holmes favored free speech but was willing to see it restricted in the emergency conditions of wartime.
   1. He wrote the majority opinion in *Schenck v. United States*, restricting antiwar and anti-conscription literature.
   2. He also upheld the conviction of socialist leader Eugene Debs, though with a rather bad conscience.
   3. In another Espionage Act case in 1919, *Abrams v. United States*, Holmes drew back, dissenting from other justices' upholding of the conviction of anarchists.

D. Holmes retired in 1932 at the age of 91 and died in 1935, having served longer than any other justice in U.S. history.
   1. As a Civil War officer, he was entitled to burial at Arlington National Cemetery.
   2. His seat on the court became known as "the scholar's seat" and was subsequently occupied by Benjamin Cardozo and Felix Frankfurter.

E. Holmes can be understood as one of the founders of *legal realism*.

Essential Reading:

Sheldon Novick, *Honorable Justice: The Life of Oliver Wendell Holmes.*

G. Edward White, *Justice Oliver Wendell Holmes: Law and the Inner Self.*

Supplementary Reading:

Mark de Wolfe Howe, *Justice Oliver Wendell Holmes*, 2 vols.

Richard A. Posner, ed. *The Essential Holmes: Selections from the Letters, Speeches, Judicial Opinions and Other Writings of Oliver Wendell Holmes.*

Questions to Consider:

1. How did Holmes's wartime experiences as a young man influence his understanding of the law and society in later life?

2. Did Holmes's decisions in World War I contradict his civil libertarian principles of the prewar and postwar years, or is it possible to see his decisions as consistent?

Lecture Thirty-Three
Henry Ford—The Mass Producer

Scope: Henry Ford (1863–1947) was another in America's long line of ingenious inventors and improvers but on a previously undreamed-of scale. He perfected a process that Eli Whitney had begun, that of mass producing identical objects, making so many that he could sell them far more cheaply than ever before. The first motor cars were toys for rich men, but Ford's Model T, first released in 1908, came steadily down in price and, by 1915, was accessible to the pocketbooks of ordinary citizens. Ford pioneered in paying high wages to production-line workers to ensure a stable workforce and to enable his men to buy the cars they were building. Ford also represents an important transition in American life that we witnessed earlier in the lives of Andrew Carnegie and Samuel Gompers: America was becoming a city-centered society, to which farming was peripheral rather than central. Ford himself, raised on a farm near Dearborn, Michigan, couldn't wait to leave the farm behind as a teenager and turn to engineering and city life. Ironically, he later romanticized farm life and other aspects of American tradition by building a quirky museum, Greenfield Village.

Outline

I. Raised in rural Michigan, the son of immigrant parents who had suffered in the Irish famine, Henry Ford early showed an aptitude for mechanical devices and gradually became familiar with the most advanced technology of his era.

    A. He served a three-year apprenticeship in Detroit and learned how to build and repair steam engines.

    B. He ran a sawmill in the late 1880s.

    C. The Edison Illuminating Company hired him in 1891, and he rose to the position of chief engineer.

II. Ford transformed the scale and character of automobile manufacturing.

    A. One of his first cars, the Quadricycle (1896), linked an internal combustion engine with four bicycle-style wheels and was steered with a tiller.

    B. Ford also built and competed in racing cars.

    C. He founded his own automobile company in 1903 on Mack Avenue in Detroit.

    D. Manufacture of the Model T began in 1908.

        1. Early assembly work was done in workshops.

        2. Borrowing a technique from the slaughterhouse industry, Ford introduced the moving assembly line in 1913.

        3. Monotony of work led to a massive turnover in his workforce.

    E. Ford introduced the $5-day in 1914, more than doubling his workmen's wages at a stroke.

        1. The work was as monotonous as before, but now the men endured the boredom for the sake of their high pay.

        2. Stability of the workforce increased the quality of the product and made line-stoppages less frequent.

        3. Ford workers could now become buyers of Ford cars.

        4. Ford also pioneered the franchised dealer system, creating an efficient sales and distribution system throughout the nation.

    F. The River Rouge Plant, developed in the early 1920s, was the world's largest and most integrated factory and employed 100,000 men.

        1. Raw materials flowed in and completed cars flowed out, at a rate of one every 40 seconds.

        2. Competition from General Motors, including cars in different colors and a stratified market, obliged Ford to abandon the Model T in 1927, by which time he had manufactured 15 million of them.

    G. In the Great Depression, Ford fought a long and bitter rear-guard action against unionization before finally accepting the United Auto Workers.

III. Ford's ideas on a variety of topics outside of auto engineering were eccentric.

    A. He made a naïve attempt to end the First World War in 1915.

        1. He chartered a ship, the *Oskar II*, and sailed it from Hoboken to Stockholm, where its passengers tried unsuccessfully to bring the belligerents into peace negotiations.

        2. When America entered the war in 1917, Ford became the "fighting pacifist," supplying the War Department with trucks, aircraft, and ships, all sold at cost.

    B. Ford was prejudiced against Jews and Catholics.

        1. He bought a newspaper, the *Dearborn Independent*, as a platform for his anti-Semitic ideas.

        2. He was widely suspected of being a Nazi sympathizer in the 1930s and early 1940s but dedicated the Willow Run plant to the building of bomber planes as a way of allaying these suspicions.

    C. He had an ambivalent view of history.

        1. Some of Ford's remarks, such as "history is bunk," implied a complete lack of interest.

        2. The founding of Greenfield Village, by contrast, suggested a fascination with the world his machines had helped make obsolete.

    D. Ford refused to become involved in a privately promoted scheme for highway building.

    E. He believed in reincarnation.

Essential Reading:

Richard Bak, *Henry and Edsel: The Creation of the Ford Empire*.

Allan Nevins and Frank Hill, *Ford: The Times, the Man, the Company*.

Supplementary Reading:

Ford R. Bryan, *Beyond the Model T: The Other Ventures of Henry Ford*.

————, *Friends, Families, and Forays: Scenes from the Life and Times of Henry Ford*.

Questions to Consider:

1. Is it surprising that Ford, despite his technical and business genius, was naïve and undereducated in most other matters?

2. Which of Ford's advances in car manufacturing and sales were most important in contributing to his overwhelming success?

Lecture Thirty-Four
Harry Houdini—The Sensationalist

Scope: As American life became more urban and more sophisticated, citizens began to crave spectacular entertainment. Buffalo Bill's Wild West—once the greatest show in the world—went into decline after 1905, upstaged by the new movie industry and by more astonishing live acts, such as Harry Houdini's escapes. Born in Hungary to Jewish parents and a childhood immigrant, Houdini (1874–1926) became a magician as a teenager but developed the ability to escape from apparently impossible situations as his specialty. Suspended upside down in chains and a straight jacket, or bound to the muzzle of a cannon with a slow-burning fuse, or plunged into a river, handcuffed and locked in a box, he learned how to wriggle free just in time and amazed crowds with his apparently impossible agility, strength, and capacity to survive. He also mastered a series of illusions, such as the ability to seemingly walk through a solid brick wall. Understanding the need to promote his acts, he adapted well to the demands of 20th-century publicity and demonstrated that show business could make a talented performer into a wealthy and influential man.

Outline

I. Erich Weiss was born in Hungary in 1874, shortly before his family's emigration to America.

   A. He was an enthusiastic gymnast, swimmer, and conjurer as a child.

   B. When the circus came to town, the 9-year-old Weiss astonished the manager with his strength and agility.

   C. As a teenager, he read the biography of a French magician, Robert-Houdin, and adopted a variant of this man's name when he began his own career as a conjurer.

   D. He went into business first with his brother, then with his wife, Beatrice Rahner, whom he married when he was just 20 and she was 18.

      1. They did card and coin tricks in a circus, and for a while, Houdini posed as a caged wild man eating raw meat.

2. Later, for the sake of variety, they posed as mediums.

3. After scattered successes in America, Houdini made a triumphant tour of Britain and Germany in 1900, after which his fame was assured.

II. Houdini began to stand out among conjurers and entertainers of his day as an escape artist.

A. The specialty that made him famous was escape from handcuffs, chains, and straight jackets, often under time duress.

1. He was fascinated by confinement and the possibility of overcoming it.

2. He first witnessed straight-jacketing at a Nova Scotia asylum and incorporated straight-jacket escapes into his act.

B. Houdini took on increasingly dangerous challenges and astonished audiences by his coolness in escaping from lethal situations.

1. Under water, in safes, and heavily chained, he nearly always escaped out of his audience's immediate line of sight.

2. Nevertheless, he had to exhibit phenomenal self-discipline.

C. He subjected himself to rigorous physical training and became immensely strong.

1. He often accomplished his feats nearly naked.

2. He taught his assistants to appear clumsy and awkward in order to deflect audiences' attention from the fact that they were actually crucial to his escapes.

D. Imprisonment and execution were morbid obsessions.

1. Houdini kept a collection of photographs of executed and mutilated prisoners.

2. He bought the first electric chair when the state of New York replaced it and kept it on display in his home.

3. One of his most famous escapes came in 1906 from the cell in which Guiteau (the killer of President Garfield) had awaited execution.

E. Houdini's success was greatest in repressive nations.

III. He took an interest not just in his own tricks but also in the history and literature of magic and magicians.

A. He published *Conjurers' Monthly Magazine* from 1906 and wrote a series of books on the history of magic.

B. He was one of many Jewish leaders in the American professional entertainment industry of the early 20th century. In 1918, he formed the Rabbis' Sons Theatrical Association. Al Jolson and Irving Berlin were members.

C. Ironically, Houdini failed in the transition to the film business.

D. He was one of the first 20th-century show business superstars, whose name became known throughout the world.

    1. His fame rivaled that of actress Sarah Bernhardt.

    2. He dedicated a good deal of his time and prestige in the 1920s to debunking psychics.

E. He died in 1926 at the age of 52, immediately after a stage performance, which he undertook despite severe pain.

    1. He was probably suffering from a burst appendix.

    2. Punches to the stomach by an admirer may have aggravated his condition.

Essential Reading:

Ruth Brando, *The Life and Many Deaths of Harry Houdini.*

Harold Kellock, *Houdini: The Life Story.*

Supplementary Reading:

J. C. Cannell, *The Secrets of Houdini.*

John Kasson, *Houdini, Tarzan, and the Perfect Man: The White Male Body and the Challenge of Modernity in America.*

Questions to Consider:

1. How did Houdini make himself stand out from among the crowd of rival sensationalists?

2. Why was the idea of witnessing escapes so attractive to crowd members?

Lecture Thirty-Five
Al Capone—The Crime Boss

Scope: Throughout American history, the names of certain criminals have taken on romantic associations. Jesse James and Billy the Kid in the 19th century and Al Capone in the 20th are cases in point. Capone (1899–1947), became the leading organized crime figure in Chicago during the 1920s, when the unpopular Prohibition Amendment to the Constitution tempted thousands of citizens to cooperate with criminals to procure alcohol. Intelligent, ruthless, but also charming and loyal, Capone organized a crime empire that dominated the city, corrupting officials at every level and in every department. He made so many people dependent on his good will that his numerous rackets and murders went unprosecuted for lack of witnesses willing to testify in court. When the Great Depression began, Capone was among the first Chicagoans to provide soup kitchens and relief supplies to the unemployed and penniless. By then, he had moved to Florida and used that fact as an alibi when members of his gang, dressed as policemen, perpetrated the St. Valentine's Day Massacre. Finally convicted not for his many violent crimes but for tax evasion, Capone spent most of the 1930s in federal prisons, emerging in 1939 to enjoy a quiet life between then and his death in 1947. The line between legitimate and shady business ventures has often been hard to draw in American history—as the example of William Mulholland also suggests—and although few can doubt that Capone stood far beyond the line, he has never entirely lacked for sympathizers.

Outline

I. Capone came from a family of Neapolitan immigrants that moved to Brooklyn in 1893.

    A. Born in 1899, Alfonse grew up in poverty and became involved in crime early, rising to leadership because of his mixture of strength, ruthlessness, business acumen, and charm.

        1. He moved to Chicago in 1919 after beating up an Irish-American gangster and joined the local Italian gangs there.

2. In Chicago, he first ran a brothel, the Four Deuces (at 2222 South Wabash Avenue), for John Torrio, a lieutenant of the local crime boss, Jim Colosimo.

3. In 1920, Torrio and Capone collaborated on assassinating Colosimo and taking control of his vice and alcohol business.

B. Torrio and Capone thrived in Chicago under Mayor "Big Bill" Thompson but found his "reform" successor, William Dever (elected 1923), far less amenable.

1. Capone moved his operations to the suburb of Cicero.

2. Torrio's severe shooting injury in 1925, followed by his retirement, enabled Capone, still in his mid-20s, to take command of a large part of the Chicago underworld.

C. Eager to restabilize the situation so that the vice trades could flourish, Capone proposed a peace treaty with his principal rival, Hymie Weiss, in 1926.

1. The volatile Weiss refused to attend and tried to kill Capone, who retaliated.

2. Capone's spokesman at the conference summarized the high death rate among bootleggers since 1920 (215 killed in inter-gang warfare and another 160 shot by police), then proposed dividing the city into bootleg districts.

3. For a time, the treaty held, but a series of high-profile gangsters' murders in 1928 led to renewed fighting.

II. Capone dominated the Chicago underworld of the late 1920s but was also a major figure in the city's public life.

A. By the late 1920s, Capone's businesses were amassing tens of millions of dollars each year.

B. Ostentatious, he drove a five-ton, armor-plated Cadillac that cost more than $30,000.

C. He displayed himself prominently at clubs, ballgames, and other public events, surrounded by bodyguards, and enjoyed being photographed and interviewed by the press.

D. During the early years of the Great Depression, he was conspicuous for his charities.

1. His soup kitchen had a reputation for cleanliness and high-quality food.

2. By persuasion and threat, he ensured that city businesses would donate food, soup, and coffee.

E. He was attentive to his mother and his wife (an Irish-American woman).

III. Capone's flagrant style prompted law enforcement agencies to pursue him.

    A. Colonel Henry Barrett Chamberlain headed the Chicago Crime Commission.

        1. He coined the term *public enemy* and called Capone "Public Enemy Number 1" and "the gorilla of gangland."

        2. Recognizing that Mayor "Big Bill" Thompson and many local politicians and law enforcers were compromised, Chamberlain sought aid from federal agents and the Treasury Department.

    B. The St. Valentine's Day Massacre, in which Capone's hired gunmen killed seven members of the rival Moran gang, outraged the public.

        1. Capone established an alibi by being in Florida that day, visiting the Miami prosecutor's office.

        2. Later, when two of the perpetrators, Scalisi and Anselmi, threatened his leadership and planned to assassinate him, Capone personally beat them to death with a baseball bat.

    C. He arranged for his own imprisonment in Philadelphia.

    D. Elliott Ness and the "untouchables" raided Capone's breweries and speakeasies.

    E. Back in Chicago, Capone was arrested in March 1931 for tax evasion.

        1. Convicted, he was sentenced to 11 years in federal prison and served first at Atlanta, then, from 1934, at San Francisco's new Alcatraz Island prison.

        2. He enjoyed none of the privileges that had made his stay in the Philadelphia prison painless.

        3. Released in 1939, mentally deranged by the effects of syphilis, Capone moved quietly to Florida and died there in 1947.

IV. Capone was the first of many celebrated leaders of American organized crime.

A. Prosecution of mobsters and congressional hearings punctuated the later 20th century.

B. Fictional Mafia bosses often appeared as romantic heroes.

    1. Mario Puzo's *The Godfather* made organized crime appear as the legitimate outcome of the Italian immigrant experience.

    2. *The Sopranos*, an HBO show of the early 21st century, also glamorized Mafia life.

Essential Reading:

Lawrence Bergreen, *Capone: The Man and the Era*.

Robert J. Schoenberg, *Mr. Capone*.

Supplementary Reading:

Luciano Iorizzo, *Al Capone: A Biography*.

George Murray, *The Legacy of Al Capone: Portraits and Annals of Chicago's Public Enemies*.

Questions to Consider:

1. What qualities enabled Capone, despite his violence and lack of education, to dominate Chicago for more than five years?

2. Why are organized crime figures attractive as well as repulsive?

Lecture Thirty-Six
Herbert Hoover—The Humanitarian

Scope: As a representative American of the late 1920s and early 1930s, few men could have been more different from Al Capone than Herbert Hoover. Most Americans remember Hoover (1874–1964) as the disastrous president who was powerless to stop the nation's slide into Depression after the Wall Street Crash of 1929 and who was swept aside by Franklin Roosevelt's triumphant New Deal. Before then, however, Hoover had been one of the most popular and widely admired men in America. He had made an excellent reputation for himself, first as a successful mining engineer and businessman in many parts of the world, then as the dominant humanitarian figure of the First World War. Belgium, invaded by German armies in 1914, was close to starvation when he intervened, bringing massive quantities of food aid from neutral America. Later, when a defeated Germany lay shattered in 1919, Hoover organized the feeding of millions more people there and throughout Central and Eastern Europe. His dedication to saving human lives and his method of ensuring efficiency, orderly management, and close accounting laid the foundations of international charity work for the rest of the 20th century. He was a distinguished politician throughout the Republican administrations of the 1920s, but the magnitude of the Depression caught him by surprise. Political opponents depicted him, quite unfairly, as cruel and indifferent to citizens' suffering and dealt a blow to his reputation from which it never recovered.

Outline

I. Hoover's early adult life was an almost unbroken succession of triumphs and achievements, despite the traumatic events of his childhood.

    A. His family, Iowa Quakers, was broken when his father died in 1880 and his mother, four years later, when he was 10.

    B. He moved to Minthorne, Oregon, where he grew up with a Quaker doctor, his mother's brother.

C. He enrolled in the then-new Stanford University in 1891 (its so-called "Pioneer Class") and graduated with a B.A. in geology in 1895.

    1. Among his summer vacation jobs was surveying work with John Wesley Powell's U.S. Geological Survey.

    2. Hoover learned the practical side of gold mining in Nevada and California, then accepted a job with a British company (Bewick Moreing) in western Australia.

    3. He showed an aptitude for identifying profitable mining sites.

D. Worldwide travel in the next 20 years brought Hoover wealth and renown, and he was a millionaire by the age of 40.

    1. The Chinese government appointed him its resident chief engineer in the Bureau of Mines.

    2. He was caught at Tientsin during the Boxer Rebellion of 1900 but helped organize resistance to the rebels.

    3. After suppression of the rebellion, he became a partner in Bewick Moreing, based in London but traveling extensively to supervise its worldwide interests.

E. As his reputation for acumen in mining, engineering, and finance grew, he created his own company in 1908, organizing new ventures and showing unprofitable ones how to become more efficient.

II. Hoover's humanitarian work in the First World War made him a national hero.

A. He helped repatriate 120,000 Americans caught in Europe and panicked by the onset of hostilities in 1914.

B. He took charge of the Commission for Relief in Belgium (CRB), trying to feed 10 million people by shipping food through naval blockades and past hostile armies.

    1. He struggled to maintain strict neutrality and declined payment for his work.

    2. Americans eventually gave more than $1 billion to finance the effort.

    3. Less than one percent was spent on administrative costs.

C. President Wilson appointed Hoover to lead the Food Administration when America entered the war directly in 1917.

D. Appealing to Americans' patriotism and idealism, he persuaded them, without coercion, to restrict their food purchases, enabling more to be sent to U.S. forces in Europe and U.S. allies.

E. As head of the American Relief Administration, Hoover managed to prevent the widespread starvation of Central Europeans immediately after the war.

    1. The conduct of the victorious Allies in trying to prevent the defeated enemy from getting food supplies disgusted him.

    2. He urged extension of aid to forestall famine in the new Soviet Union.

III. Hoover's political career flourished in the 1920s and led quickly to the White House.

A. Under Presidents Harding and Coolidge, he was Secretary of Commerce and expanded his department at a time when most areas of the federal government were shrinking.

B. He burnished his humanitarian reputation in 1927 as director of relief during the Mississippi flood crisis.

C. Elected president in 1928 over Democrat Al Smith, Hoover faced the crisis of the Wall Street Crash and the Great Depression.

    1. He lacked rhetorical gifts.

    2. He also lacked the common touch that was increasingly necessary to Democratic politicians in the radio age.

D. As the Depression worsened, Hoover expanded federal relief efforts but retained faith in voluntary and local methods of resolving the crisis.

E. Vengeful Democratic attacks and the naming of migrant workers' communities "Hoovervilles" contributed to the president's misery.

IV. Hoover, scapegoated by Democrats for his lackluster response to the Depression, became a leading critic of the New Deal and a standard-bearer for political conservatives in the 1940s and 1950s.

A. The New Deal seemed to him an attack on the American tradition of citizen independence.

    1. He criticized Roosevelt for aggregating too much power to the presidency and for using the White House as a propaganda machine.

    2. Congress, he believed, had abdicated its function to the executive.

  B. President Truman asked Hoover to lead a Famine Emergency Commission after the Second World War.

    1. He returned to work of the kind that had made him famous 30 years earlier.

    2. Presidents Truman and Eisenhower both asked him to head commissions to increase efficiency in the federal bureaucracy, and his reputation for impartiality, efficiency, and expertise revived.

    3. Hoover died in 1964, aged 90, having been an ex-president for 31 years, longer than anyone else in American history.

  C. The debate over big government continues, but Hoover's reputation has revived with the recent decline of American liberalism.

Essential Reading:

David Burner, *Herbert Hoover, a Public Life.*

George Nash, *The Life of Herbert Hoover*, 3 vols.

Supplementary Reading:

Martin L. Fausold, *The Presidency of Herbert Hoover.*

Lee Nash, ed., *Understanding Herbert Hoover: Ten Perspectives.*

Questions to Consider:

1. Did the same qualities that made Hoover an excellent engineer, businessman, and relief organizer also make him a bad president?

2. What were the motives that led Hoover to dedicate the last 50 years of his life (1914–1964) to unpaid public service?

Lecture Thirty-Seven
Helen Keller—The Inspiration

Scope: Few qualities have been more prized in American history and popular culture than the ability to overcome adversity and go on to success. Politicians learned to emphasize their humble log-cabin origins, businessmen liked to depict themselves as having risen from rags to riches, and immigrant success stories (such as Andrew Carnegie's) were based on the contrast between the humble origin and the magnificent later life. Horatio Alger tales mythologized individuals who overcame economic obstacles, but an equally strong tradition paid tribute to individuals who overcame physical challenges. None is more famous than Helen Keller (1880–1968). Daughter of an Alabama newspaper editor, she was struck blind and deaf by scarlet fever before her second birthday and seemed to have been rendered mentally defective, too. Under the care and tutelage of a gifted teacher, Anne Sullivan, however, whom she met at the age of 6, Keller learned to read, write, and make sense of the world around her. She graduated from Radcliffe College and went on to a life of advocacy on behalf of the blind, along with campaigning for women's suffrage, socialism, and other public causes. Her autobiography, *The Story of My Life* (1903), became a worldwide bestseller, and she became one of the most well known and widely recognized Americans of the 20th century.

Outline

I. Loss of both sight and hearing at the age of 18 months seemed likely to render Helen Keller incapable of literacy or an active life.

    A. The life of Laura Bridgman, however, presented the possibility that a deaf and blind child could learn to read and communicate.

        1. Bridgman's teacher, Samuel Gridley Howe, had showcased her at his Perkins School for the Blind in Boston.

        2. Around Bridgman had swirled intense psychological and theological speculation.

B. Anne Mansfield Sullivan, a graduate of the Perkins School for the Blind (valedictorian of the class of 1886), met Helen in 1887 and became her teacher.

    1. Sullivan herself was partially blind with trachoma but had recovered her sight with the help of surgery.

    2. She began spelling letters and words in Helen's hand and developed her vocabulary.

    3. In a sudden flash of inspiration at the water pump one day, Helen grasped the concept of the alphabet and of generalizations.

    4. Her senses of touch, taste, and smell were acute, which meant that she was able to alert Anne to sensations of which she had earlier been unaware.

C. Helen's rapid acquisition of language, which included learning Braille and learning to write in English, made her a child celebrity.

    1. Alexander Bell, the Perkins School, and Miss Sullivan all communicated news of Helen's achievements to the press (and exaggerated them).

    2. Helen faced an accusation of plagiarism in 1892.

    3. Mark Twain, William James, Oliver Wendell Holmes, and other leading American intellectuals befriended her.

    4. Anne Sullivan was protective of her charge and hoped to shield Helen from vulgar sensationalists.

II. Keller remained a voracious lifelong reader and became one of the most highly educated women of her era.

A. She enrolled at Radcliffe in 1900 and graduated cum laude in 1904.

    1. Sullivan continued to accompany her and facilitated her studies.

    2. During Keller's student years, she wrote a series of articles about her education. These articles were published during her sophomore year as *The Story of My Life* (1903), which became an international bestseller.

B. In 1905, Sullivan married John Macy, the Harvard instructor who had helped Keller write her autobiography. Keller went to live with them at a farmhouse in Wrentham, Massachusetts.

C. Keller became an advocate of socialism and of votes for women.

    1. Editors had an inexhaustible demand for articles about Keller's own life but were indifferent to her thoughts on politics, gender, religion, and other topics.

    2. After years of practice, she began to give public speeches in 1913.

    3. The breakup of Macy and Sullivan's marriage created a new crisis for Keller.

D. Keller planned to elope with Peter Fagan, a secretary who worked for her when Sullivan was sick, but her mother discovered and prevented the scheme.

E. Her radical and antiwar views contributed to a financial crisis, which Keller resolved by appearing in a Hollywood film about her life and by a series of vaudeville stage appearances. In these appearances, she and Sullivan recreated scenes from their lives together for fascinated audiences, as an interlude between talking parrots, gymnasts, and jugglers.

F. Anne Sullivan Macy, Keller's lifelong friend, who from the first days, she had called "Teacher," died in 1936.

    1. By then, their roles had almost been reversed, with Keller taking care of her careworn, depressed, and slightly senile old teacher.

    2. Polly Thomson, a Scottish immigrant who had lived with the family since 1914, became Keller's companion until 1960.

    3. In 1955, Keller published a biography of Sullivan, *Teacher*, describing their long and often stormy relationship.

III. Advocacy on behalf of the blind became Keller's principal concern after 1923.

    A. She was a permanent board member of the American Foundation for the Blind from its founding in 1921.

        1. She wrote and lectured on behalf of the Helen Keller Endowment Fund.

        2. The foundation was able to undertake work she strongly supported, such as standardizing Braille.

    B. After the Second World War, Keller embarked on a series of world tours, visiting blind people of 35 different nations.

IV. Keller's achievements and reputation were institutionalized in the later years of her life and after her death.

   A. Her birthplace became a museum in 1954.

   B. Keller was the subject of an Oscar-winning documentary film in 1955, *The Unconquered*, and subject of a fictional version of her life, *The Miracle Worker*, starring Anne Bancroft as Anne Sullivan and Patty Duke as Keller.

   C. President Lyndon Johnson awarded Keller the Presidential Medal of Freedom in 1964, four years before her death.

   D. Her ashes were interred at the National Cathedral in Washington, beside those of her helpers, Anne Sullivan and Polly Thomson.

   E. Her public reputation mirrored the attitude of earlier editors by emphasizing her achievement of literacy and speech more than what she did with them.

Essential Reading:

Helen Keller, *The Story of My Life*.

Joseph P. Lash, *Helen and Teacher*.

Supplementary Reading:

Dorothy Herrmann, *Helen Keller: A Life*.

Laurie Lawlor, *Helen Keller: Rebellious Spirit*.

Questions to Consider:

1. Did Anne Sullivan's need for Helen Keller become as great as Helen's for her?

2. What do Helen Keller's achievements suggest about the capacity of determined individuals to overcome severe handicaps?

Lecture Thirty-Eight
Duke Ellington—The Jazzman

Scope: Throughout its first century as an independent republic, the United States and its citizens took pride in their nation's political and economic achievements but often expressed feelings of cultural inferiority. Its writers, as we saw in the case of Emerson, had to win validation from European audiences before they could take full pride in their achievements. Before 1900, America had made few contributions to the world's musical heritage and no American musician was well known abroad. When a distinctly new and American musical form, jazz, finally drew worldwide attention, it was the music of the most despised and disadvantaged people—African-Americans. Jazz, with its roots in African rhythmical forms and the gospel/spiritual tradition, began in the bars and brothels of New Orleans and Memphis but enjoyed a countrywide vogue in the 1920s, became socially respectable, and made its greatest practitioners nationally famous. Duke Ellington (1899–1974) was among the greatest of them, a phenomenally talented pianist and composer. His rise to fame was helped not only by his musical skills but also by his good head for business and the fact that his music could be broadcast by radio, a brand-new medium in the 1920s, and by gramophone records, a second key invention. The success of Ellington's broadcasts from the Cotton Club, one of the artistic and social centers of the Harlem Renaissance, showed that white audiences loved this music, too. In the long run, the success of jazz and its celebrity musicians contributed to the decline of racial prejudice in America.

Outline

I. Born to a middle-class African-American family in Washington, DC, Edward Kennedy Ellington did not endure the childhood privations of many jazz "greats."

   A. His parents provided piano lessons, taught him table manners, and prepared him for life in the black elite.

   B. He did not take to music at first and found it difficult to read music but became much more enthusiastic after hearing ragtime.

C. Ellington encountered jazz as a teenager and created his first band, "The Duke's Serenaders," after dropping out of high school in his senior year.

    1. The high quality of the group's music ensured early success.

    2. It blended composition with improvisation, one of the principal characteristics of the new jazz.

D. Ellington had earned enough to buy his own house before the age of 20.

    1. He was also married and father of a child by then.

    2. Ellington, hard-headed and good at mathematics and organization, was the band's manager, as well as its leader and pianist.

    3. The band played throughout Washington and in the Virginia and Maryland suburbs for black and white clients.

II. Ellington became nationally famous in 1923 after moving to New York and entering its intensely competitive music scene.

A. The Harlem Renaissance of the 1920s was the first major African-American artistic movement.

    1. Ellington and other jazzmen, along with novelists, poets, and artists, made Harlem an artistic center.

    2. White admirers of this movement flocked uptown to witness Ellington and his contemporaries.

B. The recording industry, flourishing in the 1920s, enabled his band's music to be preserved and distributed nationwide.

C. Ellington's new band, "The Washingtonians," cut its first record, "Choo Choo: Gotta Hurry Home," in 1923.

D. Radio, another of the fast-growing technologies of the 1920s, gave Ellington an immense new audience.

E. Ellington's band broadcast nationwide on NBC from the Harlem Cotton Club, beginning in 1927, with such signature tunes as "East St. Louis Toodle-Oo" and the "Creole Love-Call."

F. The club had underworld connections and was patronized largely by whites.

G. Hollywood's adaptation from silent film to sound again witnessed Ellington's participation from the start. He and his music were featured in the film *Black and Tan Fantasy* in 1929.

III. Ellington was sufficiently versatile, and sufficiently aware of changing fashions, that he could adapt to new styles.

   A. His orchestra shifted to swing music in the 1930s and created one of its signature sounds, "It Don't Mean a Thing If It Ain't Got That Swing."

   B. Unlike many jazz bands of the era, Ellington's enjoyed stability of personnel and good management.

   C. He experimented with longer tunes than were normal for 78-rpm records.

   D. The band made a triumphant tour of Europe in 1933.

      1. A six-week tour of Britain was particularly successful, with the press treating Ellington as a major artistic figure.

      2. The BBC broadcast one concert, and royalty attended others.

   E. Talented band members, including Billy Strayhorn, an arranger and composer, shared many of the musical chores with Ellington. Strayhorn became a composer in his own right with "Take the 'A' Train" (1941) and other works.

   F. In 1943, Ellington's major work, "Black, Brown, and Beige," made its debut at Carnegie Hall and was the start of his work with symphonic-scale musical forces.

      1. This concert marked the first time the hall had been devoted entirely to work by a black composer, one dedicated to the role of African-Americans in the nation's history.

      2. Ellington continued to experiment with genres, moving even to liturgical music in the 1960s and early 1970s.

IV. Ellington, in his maturity, witnessed the transformation of American racial politics.

   A. Jazz musicians were among the first African-Americans to break the color line, but after World War II, many others followed.

      1. Jackie Robinson became the first black major-league baseball player (with the Dodgers) in 1947.

      2. President Truman desegregated the U.S. military in 1948.

      3. The *Brown* case of 1954 mandated desegregation of public schools and facilities.

      4. The Montgomery bus boycott (1955–1956) inaugurated the activist phase of the civil rights movement.

B. The jazzmen and other wealthy black entertainers became influential advocates for, and patrons of, civil rights activists.

C. Ellington endured criticism for not being more outspoken about civil rights, but his refusal to play to segregated audiences and the criticism of racism in his songs contributed to the transformation of American racial assumptions.

D. Musicologists began to recognize jazz as a major art form, deserving of academic study.

E. Ellington, since his death in 1974, has taken a central place in the canon of American composers.

Essential Reading:

Peter Lavezzoli, *The King of All, Sir Duke: Ellington and the Artistic Revolution.*

A. H. Lawrence, *Duke Ellington and His World: A Biography.*

Supplementary Reading:

Stuart Nicholson, *Reminiscing in Tempo: A Portrait of Duke Ellington.*

Mark Tucker, ed., *The Duke Ellington Reader.*

Questions to Consider:

1. How did the timing of Ellington's career contribute to his immense success and influence?

2. Was the existence of successful black artists, including Ellington, contributory to the transformation of American race relations after World War II?

Lecture Thirty-Nine
Charles Lindbergh—The Aviator

Scope: New inventions arrived on the American scene every year in the early 20th century, and few had more lasting importance than aircraft. The Wright brothers' experiments at Kitty Hawk showed that the powered flight of a heavier-than-air machine was feasible, which led dozens of imitators to take wing. World War I accelerated the development of aerial technology, as stronger, faster, and longer-range aircraft were developed by the warring nations. The 1920s was a decade of popular enthusiasm for flying, during which new records in racing, speed, and endurance were repeatedly established, then broken. Charles Lindbergh (1902–1974) became the most famous of these record-breakers by achieving the first solo crossing of the Atlantic Ocean in 1927 in the single-engine *Spirit of St. Louis*. Acclaimed in Europe and America for this feat, Lindbergh became an important spokesman on aviation affairs. His later life was beset with difficulties. In the early 1930s, his infant son was kidnapped and murdered. Later, he argued against American involvement in the Second World War and made isolationism a respectable posture, until the Japanese attack on Pearl Harbor. Nevertheless, Lindbergh remains an American icon of individual daring and heroism, whose act ideally linked personal willpower and technical mastery.

Outline

I. Lindbergh belonged to the first generation of Americans to grow up with aircraft.

    A. He was born in 1902, just before the Wright brothers' historic first flight.

    B. His father, a Swedish immigrant, became a Minnesota congressman between 1907 and 1917.

    C. Lindbergh attended the University of Wisconsin to study engineering.

D. After two years, he dropped out to become a barnstormer.

    1. Many surviving World War I pilots flew daredevil stunts in aerial shows for entertainment.

    2. Theorists of air travel disputed whether aircraft promised more as weapons or as harbingers of a peaceful future.

E. Lindbergh enlisted in the Army Reserve to perfect his flying skills.

F. After qualifying, he became an airmail pilot between St. Louis and Chicago.

II. His solo transatlantic flight in 1927 made Lindbergh world famous.

    A. Raymond Orteig, a New York hotelier, had offered a $25,000 prize for a non-stop crossing in 1919, but by 1927, it was still unclaimed.

        1. Alcock and Brown had previously flown together across the Atlantic from east to west.

        2. Aspirants to the Orteig prize had died in the attempt.

    B. Backed by a St. Louis businessmen's consortium, Lindbergh made his attempt in May 1927.

        1. The *Spirit of St. Louis* was a monoplane, purpose-built by Ryan Aeronautical of San Diego, with Lindbergh himself as an advisor.

        2. It set a record for trans-American travel on May 10–11.

        3. Lindbergh flew it across the Atlantic on May 20–21, taking 33 hours.

    C. Gaining instant international celebrity, Lindbergh made a goodwill tour of North and Latin America.

    D. In Mexico, he met Anne Morrow, daughter of the U.S. ambassador, and married her in 1929.

III. Lindbergh suffered personal and political turmoil in the 1930s.

    A. His son, Charles Augustus, was kidnapped in 1932 from his New Jersey home. The child was murdered by the kidnapper, Bruno Hauptmann, who later suffered the death penalty.

    B. Pestered by drama-seeking journalists, the Lindberghs moved to Europe.

        1. European aviators and governments consulted him, and he admired German aircraft development.

2. His acceptance of a medal from Hitler's air-force chief Hermann Goering in 1938 provoked an outcry from anti-Nazi Americans.

C. Lindbergh became more controversial when he represented isolationists who opposed intervention in World War II.

    1. He feared that English and Jewish organizations were maneuvering America into a war from which it could not benefit.

    2. President Franklin D. Roosevelt eventually denounced him.

D. The Japanese attack on Pearl Harbor ended Lindbergh's isolationist phase, but his reputation prevented his reenlistment in the Army Air Force.

    1. Nevertheless, as a civilian, he flew more than 50 combat missions in the Pacific Theater of the war.

    2. At the war's end, he became a consultant to the Air Force chief of staff.

IV. After World War II, Lindbergh became an elder statesman on behalf of aviation.

A. He advised manufacturers on aircraft development and airlines on suitable purchases and strategies.

    1. His 1953 autobiography, *The Spirit of St. Louis*, won the Pulitzer Prize.

    2. He cautioned against supersonic airliners because of their environmental impact.

B. After moving to Hawaii, Lindbergh also became an advocate of environmental conservation. He campaigned on behalf of endangered whale species until his death, from cancer, in 1974.

C. The example of his solo flight demonstrated to 20th-century Americans that the pioneer virtues of individualism, daring, and fortitude could be adapted to the industrial age. Careful technology and collective financing had made the venture possible, but the right individual was as important as ever before.

D. Lindbergh's life and work were major contributions to establishing the principle, more honored in America than anywhere else, that long-distance air travel was practical, safe, and effective.

Essential Reading:

A. Scott Bergh, *Lindbergh.*

Charles Lindbergh, *The Spirit of St. Louis.*

Supplementary Reading:

Von Hardesty, *Lindbergh: Flight's Enigmatic Hero.*

Dominick Pisano, *Charles Lindbergh and the Spirit of St. Louis.*

Questions to Consider:

1. How did the development of aviation technology change the character of American individualism?

2. Was Lindbergh politically naïve, or did he actually sympathize with the Nazi point of view?

Lecture Forty
Douglas MacArthur—The World-Power Warrior

Scope: Douglas MacArthur (1880–1964) was a larger-than-life army commander ideally suited to America's world-bestriding role as a superpower. Military history occasionally introduces individuals who seem always to have been in the crucial place at the crucial time; MacArthur is the perfect example. Son of an army general, a superstar at West Point, then a dashing and fearless officer during the First World War, he returned to the military academy at war's end to improve its academic profile. MacArthur rose to four-star general and chief of staff between the wars, helped eject the forlorn "Bonus Marchers" from Washington, DC, during the Great Depression, then went to the Philippines to prepare its military forces to face a growing threat from Japan. During World War II, he commanded the U.S. armies of the Pacific Theater; made a dramatic escape from Corregidor before the fall of the Philippines, while promising his men, "I will return"; then wrangled with President Roosevelt and Admiral Nimitz about how best to overwhelm the Japanese. After Hiroshima and Nagasaki, MacArthur was appointed military governor of Japan and supervised its postwar rebuilding and its political transformation into a constitutional democracy. Called back into action by the outbreak of the Korean War in 1950, he masterminded the Inchon landings, one of the most brilliant military maneuvers in history, which reversed the war's early tide of defeat. The next year, however, President Truman dismissed him when he publicly challenged the political conduct of the war, thereby violating the immensely powerful American tradition of military non-involvement in politics. The contrast between MacArthur and Francis Marion, the first American warrior we investigated in this course, parallels the contrast between America as a cluster of remote colonies struggling for independence and America as the world's premier superpower a century and a half later.

Outline

I. Son of a career army officer, MacArthur lived and breathed army life right from the beginning.

A. His father fought with a Wisconsin regiment and was a Medal of Honor winner in the Union Army of the Civil War.

    1. Douglas was born at Fort Dodge, Little Rock, Arkansas, in 1880.

    2. The elder MacArthur also fought in the Philippines during the Spanish-American War of 1898.

B. MacArthur went to West Point, where he was closely watched by his mother, who lived just off campus.

    1. He believed deeply in West Point traditions.

    2. His record as an athlete and cadet was outstanding, and he graduated first in the class of 1903, with the best record in more than 25 years.

C. Assigned to an engineering regiment, MacArthur's first combat experience came in the Philippines.

D. The First World War gave him opportunities to excel.

    1. As a brigade commander, he gained a reputation in France for impetuosity and dash, occasionally stretching or breaking his superiors' orders.

    2. He led the first American troops to reenter Sedan after its long German occupation.

II. MacArthur dominated the army of the inter-war years but was powerless to prevent deep cuts in its size and budget.

A. Not yet 40, he returned to West Point as its superintendent in 1919. He modernized its curriculum so that it could compete on even terms with the best non-military colleges of the era.

B. President Hoover appointed MacArthur chief of staff of the army in 1930, making him a four-star general.

    1. With Dwight Eisenhower as his deputy, MacArthur forcibly dispersed the "Bonus Marchers" in 1932.

    2. President Roosevelt reappointed him as chief of staff until 1935.

C. After this term, MacArthur returned to the Philippines as a military advisor and witnessed the growing power of Japan in the Pacific arena.

    1. Rather than accept a posting back in the United States in 1937, he resigned from the army and accepted command of the army of the Philippines.

2. Despite his preparations, and despite his return to the U.S. army in 1941, he was unable to repel the Japanese invasion of the Philippines after Pearl Harbor.

III. In the decade from 1942 to 1952, MacArthur became one of the most powerful men in the world but eventually overreached.

  A. Evacuated from Corregidor before its fall, he took command of the Southwest Pacific Theater.

  1. He and Admiral Chester Nimitz disputed the appropriate strategy, with MacArthur favoring recapture of the Philippines before an attack on Japan.

  2. Roosevelt accepted a scheme that incorporated elements of MacArthur's plan and elements of Nimitz's, to "leapfrog" across Pacific islands.

  B. Returning in triumph to the Philippines in 1944, MacArthur declared: "I have returned. By the grace of Almighty God our forces stand again on Philippine soil."

  C. Hiroshima and Nagasaki cut short the need for a conventional invasion of Japan.

  D. MacArthur then presided over the rebuilding of Japan, transforming it into an industrial democracy.

  1. The emperor's visit to MacArthur demonstrated their relative positions and powers.

  2. MacArthur froze out the Soviet Union from any participation in the occupation and rebuilding.

  E. North Korean attacks on South Korea in 1950 prompted a new war.

  1. President Truman gained UN authority to intervene.

  2. MacArthur's planned Inchon landings were a tactical masterpiece.

  3. His counterattack foundered when it encountered Chinese "volunteers" in North Korea.

IV. President Truman's decision in 1951 to dismiss MacArthur from his command vindicated the principle of civilian supremacy over the army.

  A. MacArthur, impatient at Truman's refusal to let him launch air strikes at targets in China, wrote a letter to a sympathetic Republican congressman that was read aloud in the House of Representatives.

B. Truman's rapid response relieved MacArthur of command.

C. He returned to the United States for the first time in 17 years and enjoyed a hero's welcome in cities across the nation.

    1. He addressed a joint session of Congress, ending with the words: "Old soldiers never die, they just fade away."

    2. He was the Republican Party's keynote speaker at its 1952 convention, but a less politically active World War II general, Eisenhower, won the nomination.

D. No military officer since MacArthur has publicly contravened the separation principle, which for more than two centuries, has safeguarded the tradition of American civil and democratic government.

Essential Reading:

Geoffrey Perrett, *Old Soldiers Never Die: The Life of Douglas MacArthur*.

Michael Schaller, *Douglas MacArthur: The Far Eastern General*.

Supplementary Reading:

Douglas MacArthur, *Reminiscences*.

William Manchester, *American Caesar: Douglas MacArthur*.

Questions to Consider:

1. What are the benefits and drawbacks of military subordination to the civil power?

2. What characteristics enabled MacArthur to rise rapidly to the top of army life and to stay there for so long?

Lecture Forty-One
Leonard Bernstein—The Musical Polymath

Scope: European music had a hierarchy of styles and types, each with an associated way of life. Classical music was one thing, jazz was another, and popular music was quite another, each with its own followers and traditions. This distinction was imported to America, but Leonard Bernstein (1918–1990) did more than anyone to break it down. A superb pianist, who was already broadcasting his own show at the age of 16, Bernstein went on to become principal conductor of the New York Philharmonic Orchestra, probably the most famous conductor in the world during the 1950s and 1960s. Determined to democratize music, however, Bernstein also stayed in touch with many other areas of the music world. He wrote several Broadway shows, of which the most famous was *West Side Story* (also a successful Hollywood film), and supported collaborations between jazz and classical musicians. Just as Duke Ellington thrived with the new technologies of radio and recording, so did Bernstein benefit from the spread of television, which coincided with his rise to fame. He appeared regularly on television throughout his prolific career, often broadcasting to children on the character of the musical classics. He had extremely high standards, yet we can appropriately see him as the man who democratized serious music.

Outline

I. Bernstein was an exceptionally precocious musician right from the start and quickly climbed to the heights of this most daunting profession.

   A. His parents, Jewish immigrants living in Lawrence, Massachusetts, feared that music might not provide a stable career.

   1. A talented scholar, the young Bernstein was educated at Boston Latin School and Harvard.

   2. From Harvard, he went to the Curtis Institute in Philadelphia to study piano, conducting, and orchestration.

   B. Serge Koussevitsky, conductor of the Boston Symphony Orchestra, recognized Bernstein's exceptional gifts when they met at Tanglewood in 1940.

      1. Bernstein became Koussevitsky's assistant, beginning a lifelong connection with the Tanglewood summer festival.

      2. He flatly refused Koussevitsky's suggestion that he change his name to Leonard S. Burns.

      3. Nevertheless, he recognized Koussevitsky as the strongest influence on his entire life and development.

C. A crucial "break" in Bernstein's career came when he met the conductor Arthur Rodzinsky, who asked him to become assistant conductor with the New York Philharmonic Orchestra.

D. Bernstein achieved nationwide fame almost overnight in 1943, when he substituted for Bruno Walter during a CBS broadcast of a concert from Carnegie Hall.

      1. He was one of the first conductors born and raised in America.

      2. In 1943, his music for the ballet *Fancy Free* was a sensational success. It broke new ground with its sense of humor and its mix of classical and jazz rhythms.

      3. From then on, Bernstein's conducting future was assured and led to his appointment as music director of the New York Symphony Orchestra in 1945.

      4. In 1958, he became music director of the New York Philharmonic and dominated it for most of the rest of his life.

E. Bernstein overcame America's reputation for musical provincialism by becoming the first American to conduct the London Symphony, the Berlin Philharmonic, and opera at La Scala in Milan.

F. He also championed the music of such American composers as Aaron Copland, Charles Ives, and Samuel Barber.

II. While establishing himself as one of the world's leading conductors, Bernstein also excelled in a variety of other musical genres, was always lively, and was often controversial.

A. His score for the film *On the Waterfront* (1954) won an Oscar nomination.

B. He wrote a series of Broadway musicals.

      1. The first, *On the Town* (1944), was popular among wartime audiences.

2. The most famous, *West Side Story* (1957), written with Jerome Robbins and Stephen Sondheim, became an Oscar-winning movie in 1961.

C. Bernstein's symphonic compositions won high critical regard but also many sharply negative reactions.

1. The symphonies' titles, *Jeremiah* (#1) and *Kaddish* (#3), bore witness to his refusal to disguise his Jewish identity.

2. Nevertheless, he produced a superb setting of the traditional Catholic mass, which some critics acclaimed a masterpiece (and others dismissed as "derivative and attitudinizing drivel").

D. Television appealed to Bernstein as a medium through which he might bring classical music to a wider audience, particularly to children. For 15 seasons, beginning in 1958, he hosted *Young People's Concerts* on CBS TV.

E. Bernstein excelled in many forms of teaching and, in 1973, delivered an erudite lecture series on the character of music at Harvard. The series was later published as *The Unanswered Question*.

III. A series of political (sometimes naïve) enthusiasms, generally on the liberal left, provoked controversy, especially during the volatile 1960s, but could not dent Bernstein's overwhelmingly positive reputation.

A. His unswerving support for Israel made him a national hero there, as well as a popular guest conductor.

B. He hosted parties for various radical causes in the 1960s.

1. He became an outspoken opponent of America's role in the Vietnam War.

2. When Bernstein and his wife hosted a party on behalf of the Black Panthers, the social critic Tom Wolfe satirized him in the famous article "Radical Chic."

C. Bernstein led the European Community Youth Orchestra on a "Journey for Peace" concert tour, including concerts in Athens and Hiroshima.

D. His conducting of concerts on both sides of the Berlin Wall as it was dismantled in 1989 demonstrated his recognition of the moment's symbolic importance.

E. Aspects of Bernstein's legacy include a wider democratic appreciation for classical music and a characteristically American attempt to dismantle the barriers that separate musical styles and genres.

Essential Reading:

Paul Myers, *Leonard Bernstein*.

Meryle Secrest, *Leonard Bernstein: A Life*.

Supplementary Reading:

Leonard Bernstein, *The Unanswered Question: Six Talks at Harvard*.

Humphrey Burton, *Leonard Bernstein*.

Questions to Consider:

1. How did Bernstein exploit the technological innovations of his era to popularize music?

2. Was the development of a distinguished American tradition in classical music the logical accompaniment of America's rise to world-power status?

Lecture Forty-Two
Shirley Temple—The Child Prodigy

Scope: European visitors to America in the 19th and early 20th centuries, especially from Britain, were surprised at Americans' commitment to equality and democracy. Many of them were even more surprised by Americans' methods of bringing up children, which seemed to them excessively permissive, encouraging too much precocity too early in life. They often found American children noisy and boisterous. Others noted the simultaneous American tendency to idealize children and childhood. No child better embodied the ideas of youthful independence and innocent virtue than Shirley Temple (born 1928). On the stage before the age of 3, she won a part in a mainstream movie in 1934 and became, almost at once, a spectacular success. Shirley Temple was the most popular attraction in Hollywood for four consecutive years, made 40 films before her 12th birthday, and became an iconic figure of good will and good cheer in the midst of the Great Depression. Her sensational film success, however, could not be duplicated in later life, and after a few films in her teens, she left Hollywood. Nationally famous, however, she later became active in Republican Party affairs with her businessman-husband and served a succession of administrations as an ambassador, State Department officer, and White House protocol chief. Temple's experience of overwhelming success in early childhood has rarely been matched, though more recent generations of ice skaters and gymnasts have also achieved greatness early in life, often at the cost of ordinary childhood.

Outline

I.   An ambitious stage mother pushed the infant Shirley straight into the limelight and kept her there.

    A. Her father was a Santa Monica bank teller and her mother, a housewife and stage mother.

    B. Shirley began her film career in the *Baby Burlesques*, parodies of current movies played by 3- to 5-year-old children, some still in diapers.

1. As a 4-year-old, Shirley could perform effective imitations of Marlene Dietrich and Mae West.
2. Passage of the Hayes Office's movie production code ended the burlesques.
C. Shirley's first studio film was *Stand Up and Cheer* (1934), the success of which amazed Twentieth Century Fox.
   1. It and its successors enabled the studio to rebound from near bankruptcy.
   2. Studio chief Darryl Zanuck lent Temple his personal bodyguard.
   3. Temple won an Oscar for her role in *Bright Eyes*.

II. Twentieth Century Fox marketed the Temple phenomenon aggressively.
   A. A succession of films was written especially for her in 1935–1939.
      1. Her character was playful, resourceful, loving, honest, and free of adult prejudices and foibles.
      2. Her ability as a song and dance artist led to her pairing with "Bojangles" Robinson in *The Little Colonel*, at a time when cross-racial scenes in film were almost unknown.
   B. More than a million Shirley Temple dolls sold in each year of the late 1930s.
   C. Temple also endorsed lines of breakfast cereal, soap, and clothes.
   D. President Franklin Roosevelt paid tribute to her "infectious optimism."

III. Declining enthusiasm after 1940 led Temple to realize that her popularity had depended on her exceptional ability in early youth.
   A. She married John Agar, an aspiring film star, as a 17-year-old but was divorced by the age of 21.
      1. When she remarried, it was to a businessman, Charles Black, with whom she turned her interests to public service.
      2. Her only sustained stint before the cameras as an adult came in 1958–1961, when she hosted a children's television series.
   B. Temple-Black's intelligence, poise, and popularity made her an attractive choice for diplomatic appointments in later years.
      1. She was outspoken on several controversial issues, taking a strongly conservative line.

2. President Nixon made her U.S. representative to the United Nations in 1969, when she was still only 40.

3. In 1974, Temple accepted President Ford's appointment to be American ambassador in Ghana, then to be the first female White House chief of protocol.

4. As American ambassador to Czechoslovakia for the first President George Bush, she witnessed the "Velvet Revolution" of 1989.

C. Temple-Black also headed a series of charities, following her brother's diagnosis with multiple sclerosis in 1952.

D. Her decision to publicize the fact that she was suffering from breast cancer in 1972 contributed to a transformed attitude to this affliction among American women. Her recovery demonstrated the importance of regular checks, early intervention, and widespread education on the issue.

IV. Child stars have remained both popular and controversial in America since Shirley Temple's heyday in the 1930s.

A. Other film child stars, such as Judy Garland, Drew Barrymore, and Macaulay Culkin, missed out on conventional childhood and found it difficult, subsequently, to adapt to adult roles.

B. The premature forcing of child superstars in athletics and ice-skating also raised troubling questions about the possibility of exploitation. The child stars' profitability and attractiveness often offset the promoters' qualms.

Essential Reading:

Jean Blashfield, *Shirley Temple Black: Actor and Diplomat.*

Shirley Temple, *Child Star: An Autobiography.*

Supplementary Reading:

Patsy Guy Hammontree, *Shirley Temple Black: A Bio-Bibliography.*

Norman Zierold, *The Child Stars.*

Questions to Consider:

1. Was Shirley Temple's phenomenal success attributable to the fact that she was such a tonic to Depression-era conditions?

2. Are ambitious parents justified in promoting their young children's show-business or athletic careers when the children themselves are incapable of making rational decisions about them?

Lecture Forty-Three
George Wallace—The Demagogue

Scope: Democratic political systems are always vulnerable to demagogues, men who take advantage of the system to preach hatreds or rouse the population on behalf of twisted and distorted versions of the truth. There is a shabby tradition of demagogy in American history, which reached one of its low points in the 1950s and 1960s, first with Senator Joseph McCarthy, who cynically manipulated the issue of anticommunism, then with Governor George Wallace of Alabama. At a time when the civil rights movement was trying to break down the racial segregation system, Wallace (1919–1998) built his political career on uncompromising opposition to integration. Alleging that integration of schools would bring sexual promiscuity, degradation, and decline, he generated an electric response among Alabama's white voters. Impressed by his own success, he took the same message onto the national stage in his controversial run for the presidency in 1968, combining the manipulation of racist imagery with pro-Vietnam War, anti-radical rhetoric. His third-party candidacy that year won more votes than any other in American history and prompted him to try again in 1972. An assassination attempt, however, ended these presidential aspirations and appears to have transformed his outlook more broadly. By the early 1980s, Wallace had reinvented himself as an Alabama leader for all races and had swept back into power with the help of black voters as well as white.

Outline

I.   In his early career, Wallace was distinctly less racist than some of his opponents.

   A. Wallace was born in 1919 and raised on a farm in Barbour County.

   B. As a 17-year-old, he became the state's high-school bantamweight boxing champion.

      1. He entered the University of Alabama the next year and continued to box for money to help pay his fees.

2. He graduated from University of Alabama's law school in 1942.

C. Wallace served a brief stint in the Army Air Force, despite health problems. He flew nine combat missions over Japan but was given a discharge on grounds of health.

D. Elected to the state assembly in 1946, he showed a flair for populist politics. In 1949, he joined the trustees of Booker T. Washington's Tuskegee Institute.

E. A Democratic Party loyalist, Wallace was elected circuit court judge in 1953.

II. The civil rights movement created a backlash among white southern voters that Wallace rode to state (and almost national) power.

A. Defeated in his first bid for the state's governorship in 1958, Wallace realized that his opponent, John Patterson, had made better use of the segregation issue than he and vowed not to be "out-segged" again.

B. In 1962, he won an overwhelming victory as state governor, posing as the champion of segregation.

   1. Wallace created a dramatic confrontation at the University of Alabama in 1963, preventing the enrollment of its first black students.

   2. Police violence against civil rights demonstrators in Birmingham (1963) and on the Selma-Montgomery march (1965) made Wallace's state notorious for its ferocious defense of segregation.

C. Precluded by the state's constitution from running for a second term as governor, Wallace persuaded his wife, Lurleen, to stand in for him in 1966. She did, and she won. She died of cancer during her term of office.

D. Wallace himself ran for president in 1968 as an independent candidate against Nixon (R) and Humphrey (D).

   1. His campaign exploited the dissatisfied working-class white majority.

   2. He criticized "pointy-headed intellectuals" and Washington bureaucrats.

3. His was, to that point, the most successful third-party candidacy in American history.

E. Reelected governor of Alabama in 1970, Wallace had an acute sense of how to manipulate the public mood.

    1. A second presidential bid seemed likely to be even more successful in 1972.

    2. Shot by Arthur Bremer during the Maryland primary campaign, Wallace was paralyzed and had to abandon the race.

    3. A constitutional change enabled him to win a third gubernatorial term in 1974, but a further presidential bid soon fizzled.

III. In the 1980s, Wallace declared that his earlier manipulation of race had been mistaken, after which he reinvented his political career on the basis of racial inclusiveness.

A. He won a fourth term as governor in 1982.

    1. In a speech to the Southern Christian Leadership Conference, he described his earlier segregationist policies as having been wrong.

    2. He won majorities in all 10 of Alabama's majority-black counties.

B. Wallace governed with an effective alliance of organizations representing blacks, educators, and organized labor.

Essential Reading:

Dan T. Carter, *The Politics of Rage: George Wallace, the Origins of the New Conservatism, and the Transformation of American Politics.*

Marshall Frady, *Wallace: The Classic Portrait of Alabama Governor George Wallace.*

Supplementary Reading:

Michael Dorman, *The George Wallace Myth.*

Stephen Lesher, *George Wallace: American Populist.*

Questions to Consider:

1. Why did so many white voters, in the North and South, find Wallace an attractive candidate in the late 1960s and early 1970s?

2. Is it reasonable to believe that Wallace's racial "conversion" was sincere?

Lecture Forty-Four
William F. Buckley, Jr.—The Conservative

Scope: Throughout the 19th century, America was world famous as the revolutionary leader that had thrown off monarchy, declared itself a constitutional republic, and made its theoretical system work in practice. It had inspired the French and Latin American revolutions of the following decades and won the admiration of radicals in every European nation. After the Russian Revolution, however, America began to represent the forces of world conservatism, battling against the dangerous radicalism that communism had come to represent. Americans had generally been reluctant to call themselves conservatives, at least until the mid-20th century. William F. Buckley, Jr. (born 1925) was among the first Americans to take pride in the conservative label, and he helped to turn conservative ideas into practical political realities between 1950 and the 1980s. He founded *National Review* magazine in 1955, gathering disparate groups of anticommunists, classical liberals, and social traditionalists and offering them a place to work out the practical implications of their ideas. A gifted publicist and a powerful debater, Buckley soon became a television personality, too, and for three decades, hosted *Firing Line*, a conservative interview and talk show. The vindication of his life's work came with the election of 1980, when Ronald Reagan, an outspokenly conservative Republican, became president, having seemed, just a decade earlier, far too right-wing ever to achieve the highest office. Buckley transformed the image and idiom of conservatism, with consequences that persisted into the 21st century.

Outline

I. Born to a wealthy Catholic family in 1925, William enjoyed an exceptionally privileged childhood during the Great Depression but, from the beginning, made the most of his advantages.

    A. His father had made his fortune in the oil business.

    B. William went to boarding schools in New England and old England.

C. The family's business interests in Latin America led to a bilingual childhood.

D. After a brief stint in the army, Buckley attended Yale.

    1. He edited the *Yale Daily News*.

    2. On graduation, he published the controversial *God and Man at Yale*, an indictment of the university for what he described as its atheism and socialism.

E. His next book, *McCarthy and His Enemies*, co-written with L. Brent Bozell, was the only intellectually plausible defense of the demagogue Wisconsin senator.

II. *National Review*, which Buckley launched in 1955, gathered together America's disparate conservative intellectuals to make a sustained assault on the era's liberal orthodoxy.

A. From the beginning, the publication's contributors were militant anticommunists.

    1. Contributors included such former communists as Max Eastman, James Burnham, and Whittaker Chambers, who now regarded communism as the great threat to Western civilization.

    2. "Classical liberals," such as Henry Hazlitt, also participated.

    3. Religious, especially Catholic, contributors included Buckley, Bozell, and the young Garry Wills, a Jesuit seminarian.

B. Buckley was careful to exclude racist fanatics and conspiracy theorists.

C. Early editions supported the Montgomery bus boycott but ridiculed the novelist Ayn Rand.

D. Buckley's ability to make the journal entertaining and lively brightened the sober image of American conservatism for the first time in the 20th century.

E. *National Review* campaigned against any "thaw" in the Cold War and was disappointed by the defeat of its first presidential favorite, Barry Goldwater, in 1964.

F. *NR* editor Bozell (Buckley's brother-in-law) ghost-wrote Goldwater's *The Conscience of a Conservative*.

G. Reaction against the social upheavals of the 1960s brought growing numbers of former liberals into the conservative camp: the *neo-conservatives*.

III. Buckley's success as a debater and media personality made him, by the mid-1960s, the living personification of American conservatism.

    A. Buckley's New York mayoralty campaign in 1965 enlarged his media appeal.

    B. It was the basis of his bestseller, *The Unmaking of a Mayor* (1966).

    C. *Firing Line*, a conservative talk show and debate arena, kept Buckley constantly before a wide, educated public from 1966 to 1999.

        1. He had been a champion debater at Yale.

        2. Famous political, literary, musical, and scholarly guests provided controversy and entertainment.

    D. Buckley gathered admirers for his hobbies and interests, as well as for his political views.

        1. A talented yachtsman, he wrote compelling books about ocean crossings.

        2. Devoutly Catholic, he was dismayed by changes in his church during the 1960s in the wake of the Second Vatican Council.

        3. In the 1980s and 1990s, he also cranked out a succession of lively pot-boiling espionage novels.

IV. Ronald Reagan brought to the White House ideas Buckley had been preaching and publicizing for 25 years and vindicated many of his most deeply cherished beliefs.

    A. Reagan's "evil empire" rhetoric about the Soviet Union mirrored Buckley's own.

    B. Buckley took pleasure in witnessing the collapse of the Soviet empire at the end of the 1980s.

    C. Buckley shared (and educated) many conservative politicians' concerns about family breakup, religious decline, drugs, and delinquency.

    D. The politics of the 1980s exposed the fissure in conservatives' ranks between the principles of *laissez faire* and the need for government guidance at a moment of social crisis.

E. America's retreat from the interventionist liberalism of the 1960s and the breakup of the Democratic Party's mid-century New Deal coalition gratified Buckley.

F. By the turn of the millennium, he could regard conservatism as the dominant political and social philosophy of the entire United States, a condition he had done much to stimulate.

Essential Reading:

John Judis, *William F. Buckley, Jr.: Patron Saint of the Conservatives.*

George Nash, *The Conservative Intellectual Movement in America Since 1945.*

Supplementary Reading:

Patrick Allitt, *Catholic Intellectuals and Conservative Politics in America, 1950–1985.*

William F. Buckley, Jr., *The Unmaking of a Mayor.*

Questions to Consider:

1. What combination of political and personal skills enabled Buckley to build an effective conservative movement after 1950?

2. Were foreign or domestic issues more important in Buckley's analysis of the Cold War world and America's role in it?

Lecture Forty-Five
Roberto Clemente—The Athlete

Scope: Throughout the 20th century, the world of entertainment offered an avenue of advancement to members of racial and ethnic minorities, as we have seen in the case of several Jewish and African-American figures. Athletics was another way by which poor and obscure young Americans could rise to national fame. Roberto Clemente (1934–1972) was among the greatest of them. An outstanding athlete, Clemente became a major-league prospect in the early 1950s and went on to play his entire 17-year major-league career with the Pittsburgh Pirates. He was, however, a Puerto Rican, whose country had been annexed by the United States during the Spanish-American War of 1898–1900 after four centuries of Spanish occupation. During Clemente's childhood, Puerto Rico's independence movement was repressed by the U.S. government, fearful lest an independent Puerto Rico join the communist side in the Cold War. Independence extremists attempted to assassinate President Truman in 1950 and machine-gunned members of Congress in 1954. Clemente, by contrast, became the best known and most admired Puerto Rican in America in the late 1950s and through the 1960s, aware that he had the power to influence other Americans' opinions of his country for good or ill. He complemented his skills in baseball with an energetic role in humanitarian work, gradually emerging as an exceptionally positive symbolic figure. Clemente's death in 1972, while taking part in an earthquake-relief operation, sealed his reputation as the ideal role model to American boys from the nation's sports history.

Outline

I. Clemente's early life pointed directly to an exceptional sporting career.

    A. He was born in Barrio San Anton in Carolina, Puerto Rico, during the Great Depression.

        1. He grew up in poverty but excelled in sprinting, javelin, and baseball as a high school student.

2. He joined a Puerto Rican winter-league baseball team, the Juncos, from high school.
3. The Brooklyn Dodgers drafted him to the Montreal farm team, the Royals, in 1953.

B. The Pittsburgh Pirates acquired Clemente in the 1954 minor-league draft for $4,000. He played right field for the Pirates in 1955 and held onto the opening spot in that position for the next 17 years.

C. Clemente helped turn an ailing Pirates team into a major National League force by 1960. He batted over .300 for eight consecutive years and played in the World Series of 1960.

D. In the 1960s, he won all the major batting and fielding awards, including 12 Gold Gloves, and was a regular All-Star.
1. He won the National League's batting title four times, in 1961, 1964, 1965, and 1967.
2. He was the National League's Most Valuable Player in 1966, a year in which he hit 119 RBI and 29 homeruns.

II. Clemente was obliged to shoulder the burden of representing Puerto Rico among other Americans, whether or not he wanted to.

A. Puerto Rico, annexed by the United States in 1900, enjoyed a thriving independence movement in the inter-war years.
1. Recurrent violence between pro- and anti-independence political factions marked the Depression years.
2. Standards of living were much lower than in the United States.

B. The logic of American anti-imperialism during World War II pointed toward early independence.
1. Rising anticommunist fears in the early Cold War era, however, pointed to continued Puerto Rican attachment to the United States.
2. Large-scale Puerto Rican migration to New York and other parts of the United States began after World War II.
3. Congress authorized Puerto Ricans' election of their own governor in 1948 and made the island a self-governing commonwealth within the United States in 1950.

C. Radical Puerto Rican nationalists attempted to assassinate President Truman in 1950 and attacked congressmen with guns in 1954.

D. Clemente, touchy and proud, sometimes balked against the expectation that he should embody Puerto Rican identity.

   1. He was obliged to play the same role among Hispanic players that Jackie Robinson and other pioneering African-American major-leaguers had had to play.

   2. He would take himself out of the lineup when hurt, despite criticism that he was a hypochondriac.

   3. Other Puerto Ricans began to figure in American popular culture, such as the characters in *West Side Story* and the musician Jose Feliciano.

III. Clemente's durability as a dependably first-class star player, and his steady emergence as one of the most popular athletes in America, soothed earlier tensions, while his untimely death transformed him into a symbol of the citizen-athlete.

A. The last years of his playing career were among his best.

   1. Clemente batted .414 in the 1971 World Series for the championship-winning Pirates and was elected Series MVP.

   2. On the last day of the 1972 season, he made his 3,000th hit, becoming only the 11th player in history to reach this milestone.

B. On New Year's Eve 1972, he flew with a planeload of relief supplies to Managua, Nicaragua, to help earthquake victims. The plane crashed within five miles of takeoff, killing Clemente and four others.

C. Major League Baseball, Pittsburgh, and other organizations have subsequently honored his name and memory.

   1. He was inducted into the Hall of Fame almost at once (1973), following a waiver of the normal five-year rule.

   2. The National League batting title was subsequently named for him.

   3. Pittsburgh's Twelfth Street Bridge was renamed the Roberto Clemente Bridge.

Essential Reading:

Bruce Markusen, *Roberto Clemente: The Great One.*

Charles E. Mercer, *Roberto Clemente.*

Supplementary Reading:

Arnold Hanno, *Roberto Clemente: Batting King.*

Nancy Morris, *Puerto Rico.*

Questions to Consider:

1. Is it possible for a man in Clemente's situation to avoid the burden of becoming a national symbol?

2. Which is the more significant story: prejudice against Puerto Ricans among other Americans or the gradual overcoming of such prejudice?

Lecture Forty-Six
Betty Friedan—The Feminist

Scope: During the Revolutionary War, Abigail Adams wrote her husband to "remember the ladies." Throughout American history, groups of educated women expressed the belief that men denied them the right to participate fully in the nation's life. A first feminist movement worked hard for women's votes before and after the turn of the 20th century and saw their work crowned with success when the Nineteenth Amendment guaranteed women's suffrage in 1920. A second wave of feminism broke over the nation in the 1960s and 1970s. The galvanizing event setting it in motion was publication of Betty Friedan's book *The Feminine Mystique* (1963), a sweeping indictment of women's lives in postwar America. Friedan herself (b. 1921) was a Smith College graduate, social radical, and investigative journalist, who found she had struck a resonant chord when her book became a great bestseller. She founded the National Organization of Women (NOW) in 1966 and became one of the two or three central figures in the successful campaign to abolish discriminatory legislation. A powerful and combative figure, she struggled with such rival feminist leaders as Gloria Steinem and Bella Abzug in the 1970s but continued to work on a variety of issues relating to sexuality, politics, childcare, and abortion. In the 1990s, her writings also contributed to a growing debate about aging in America.

Outline

I. Born Betty Naomi Goldstein in 1921, Friedan spent much of her youth in the radical political left.

    A. Born and raised in Peoria, Illinois, as the daughter of Jewish immigrants, Friedan went east to college at Smith, graduating in the class of 1942.

    B. She began the doctoral program in psychology at the University of California, Berkeley, but abandoned it and moved to New York.

C. During and after World War II, she worked as a radical journalist in New York.
  1. A recent biographer's discovery that she had been a communist shone a new light on her critical attitude to American institutions.
  2. Friedan worked for the Federated Press, a radical news service, from 1943–1946.
D. Unhappily married to Carl Friedan, she began, in the 1950s, to investigate the lives of her former Smith College classmates and found that many of them also were dissatisfied with their materially privileged but stultifying suburban lives.
E. These insights formed the basis of *The Feminine Mystique* (1963), a wide-ranging critique of gender relations in America, which mixed anecdotes from her own life with criticism of American assumptions and academic orthodoxies.
  1. It argued that women were unable to actualize their own identities and had to live vicariously through the achievements of their husbands and children.
  2. The book criticized the gender bias in Freudian psychoanalysis.
  3. It described the middle-class woman's home as a "comfortable concentration camp."
  4. It included a sharp indictment of advertising, child-rearing literature, and popular cultural presentations of women's lives.

II. Friedan founded NOW to lobby against gender discrimination in the economy, which she saw as the most important arena for feminism.
A. NOW's lobbying led to the writing of most legislation in gender-neutral language.
  1. Friedan also recognized that access to childcare was essential if women were to play a larger role in the workforce—she tried to make childcare tax deductible and to have it provided by the federal government.
  2. Friedan organized the Women's Strike for Equality in 1970 on the 50th anniversary of the Nineteenth Amendment.
  3. She founded the National Women's Political Caucus in 1971 and campaigned to elect more women to public offices.

4. She also supported the pro-choice position in the abortion controversy and welcomed the Supreme Court's *Roe v. Wade* decision in 1973.

B. The more radical "women's liberation" movement favored "consciousness raising" and a transformed attitude to sexual politics.

    1. Friedan, divorced in 1969 after a stormy marriage, was not oblivious to such issues.

    2. She became concerned lest sexuality questions (especially those relating to lesbianism) distract the movement from its principal areas of political and economic emphasis.

    3. She witnessed, and wrote perceptively about, the fragmentation of "second-wave" feminism.

    4. She shared the widespread feminist regret at the failure of the Equal Rights Amendment to win ratification from the states.

C. Friedan became a director of the First Women's Bank and Trust Company in 1973, an attempt to practice feminist principles in the economy.

III. Slightly ahead of the Baby Boom generation in age, Friedan was an early advocate for the valuable role that aging citizens could play in late 20th-century America.

A. Her book *The Fountain of Age* (1993) deplored the tendency to set aside the value of aging people and argued for their continuing vitality.

B. On the national lecture circuit, Friedan became an advocate for the growing elderly sector of American society.

Essential Reading:

Betty Friedan, *The Feminine Mystique*.

Daniel Horowitz, *Betty Friedan and the Making of the Feminine Mystique: The American Left, the Cold War, and Modern Feminism*.

Supplementary Reading:

Judith Hennessee, *Betty Friedan: Her Life*.

Rosalind Rosenberg, *Divided Lives: American Women in the Twentieth Century*.

Questions to Consider:

1. Was it the style or the content of *The Feminine Mystique* that made it so compelling to readers in the early 1960s?

2. Why did the second wave of American feminism become so fragmented after 1970, and was Friedan in part responsible?

Lecture Forty-Seven
Jesse Jackson—The Civil Rights Legatee

Scope: Martin Luther King, Jr., was not a politician. His uncompromising resistance to segregation forced the system to change, but he did it from the outside, refusing to make the kind of concessions inevitable and necessary among practicing politicians. Jesse Jackson (b. 1941), by contrast, has led a career half in and half out of ordinary politics. Present at the assassination of King in 1968, he inherited the mantle of leadership of the civil rights movement. Another minister, Jackson sometimes emulated King's method of preaching righteous judgment against a sinful society. At other times, however, he tried to become directly involved in electoral politics, running twice for president in the 1980s. These attempts obliged him to build alliances and enter into the give and take of the political process, along with its many moral gray areas. He discovered, during his "Rainbow Coalition" campaigns, that he could raise enough money and electoral support to challenge Democratic Party orthodoxy but not enough to win the party's nomination or a nationwide election. This dilemma marked most of Jackson's career, as did his alternation between criticizing white racism on the one hand and urging black economic self-help on the other. In him was symbolized much of the heritage of such earlier African-American leaders as Booker T. Washington and King, a heritage he tried to put to good use in the era after the abolition of legally enforced segregation.

Outline

I. Jackson, from early in life, aspired to academic, sporting, and leadership distinction.

    A. He was stigmatized as illegitimate in childhood. His mother was a 17-year-old high-school dropout when he was born, and his father was her married neighbor.

    B. Excelling in school, Jackson encountered racial obstacles in his pursuit of academic and athletic distinction.

1. An athletic scholarship student at the University of Illinois (1959), he believed he was denied the role of starting quarterback because of his race.
2. Enrolling instead at North Carolina A&T State University, a historically black school, he became quarterback and president of the student body.
3. He became an activist in the Congress of Racial Equality as it struggled to overturn local segregation ordinances.

C. As a theological student at Chicago Theological Seminary after college, he studied theology and practiced oratory before ordination to the Baptist ministry.

1. He dropped out of seminary in 1966 to work full-time with the Southern Christian Leadership Conference (SCLC) and guided King around its projects in Chicago.
2. He witnessed King's shooting in Memphis in 1968 and was among those present at the leader's death.

II. Tensions among King's heirs prompted Jackson to strike out on his own after 1970, blending a lesson of black self-help and anti-racism.

A. Jackson feuded with Ralph Abernathy, King's old lieutenant, about the SCLC's future direction.

B. Jackson's new organization, People United to Save Humanity (PUSH), helped energize black businesses, workers, and homeowners in Chicago, giving them a fuller place in the city's economy.

1. Critics regarded its methods as coercive against Chicago businessmen.
2. PUSH-EXCEL helped black students stay in school until graduation.

C. His widespread recognition prompted Jackson to mount a presidential bid in 1984.

1. His "Rainbow Coalition" aimed to unite a wide variety of racial and ethnic minorities, along with poor whites and other disadvantaged citizens.
2. Strong showing in several primaries enabled Jackson to influence the Democratic Party platform under candidate Walter Mondale.
3. However, his campaign faltered under accusations of anti-Semitism, provoked by his pro-Palestinian stance and his

friendship with Louis Farrakhan, leader of the Nation of Islam. Matters were not helped by his use of an anti-Jewish slur.

D. A stronger presidential bid in 1988 was based on an array of programs further to the political left than those favored among mainstream Democrats.

    1. Jackson argued for a national housing program, women's wage parity, higher minimum wages, and drastic anti-drug policies.

    2. He was again strong enough to win numerous primaries and influence the national ticket but could not take the nomination itself from Michael Dukakis.

    3. Jackson's association with the Nation of Islam's Elijah Muhammad, an anti-Semite, blighted his reputation for exemption from prejudice.

III. In the 1990s, an older Jesse Jackson, by then the nation's African-American elder statesman, became involved in a variety of important and high-profile national projects.

A. He played the role of diplomat extraordinary for several presidents.

    1. He brought a group of American hostages out of Kuwait in 1990.

    2. He also secured the release of three American soldiers captured by the Yugoslav tyrant Slobodan Milosevic in 1999.

    3. He played a recurrent role in the struggle for Middle Eastern peace accords.

B. As the District of Columbia's "statehood senator," Jackson campaigned against the anomaly that denied the district any representation in Congress.

C. After 1997, Jackson's "Wall Street Project" attempted to influence race relations in the nation's leading corporations. In what Jackson described as the move from "sharecroppers to shareholders," he believed minorities should participate directly in the direction of America's capitalist institutions.

Essential Reading:

Marshall Frady, *Jesse: The Life and Pilgrimage of Jesse Jackson.*

Arnold Gibbons, *Race, Politics and the White Media: The Jesse Jackson Campaigns*.

Supplementary Reading:

Marable Manning, *Black American Politics: From the Washington Marches to Jesse Jackson*.

Kenneth Timmerman, *Shakedown: Exposing the Real Jesse Jackson*.

Questions to Consider:

1. In what ways did Jackson enjoy advantages in his leadership of the African-American community by comparison with King?

2. Were greater successes possible for the Rainbow Coalition, or was it destined to be no more than an influential minority in the Democratic Party?

Lecture Forty-Eight
Stability and Change

Scope: A course of this type has no logical beginning or end. It would certainly be possible to outline the lives of dozens more famous and fascinating Americans, explaining the significance of their work and the meaning of their lives to the nation and its development. In the selection of the 50 or so men and women we have studied over the last 47 lectures, comprehensiveness was impossible, and many subjects deserving of far more attention were neglected or, at least, scanted. Just to give an obvious example, the only scientists described lived before 1800. It would certainly have been possible to say a great deal about the succession of Nobel Prize–winning scientists who brought luster to the nation, especially in the years after World War II, similarly with far more artists and writers than we had the chance to discuss.

Given that the course is impressionistic rather than comprehensive, this lecture attempts to summarize some of the ideas we have developed about American identity as a whole, returning to points raised in Lecture One but now with more illustrative material to enrich our survey. This lecture also underlines a point made at the outset of the course. Although it is possible to describe certain traits and characteristics as distinctly American, this is not to imply that they are part of a prescription. Neither are these characteristics unchanging. Our job, in this last lecture, is to see how certain themes and ideas have persisted and how others, in such a dynamic society, have changed beyond recognition.

Outline

I. Commitment to human equality and to democratic government is among the constants we can trace throughout this history, though at different times, *equality* and *democracy* have themselves been defined in different ways.

A. When Abigail Adams asked her husband to "remember the ladies" as the project of governing America was reconceived, she was joking, but her feminist heirs were serious and had their way. Betty Friedan justified her work in terms of giving women real equality and real democratic access, rather than merely the outward legal shell, when it was clear that votes for women had not been enough.

B. Jefferson was serious about equality, but he was also an active slaveholder and slave-code writer.

    1. The work of Frederick Douglass showed that equality and slaveowning were incompatible and that the abolition of slavery was a moral imperative.

    2. Two generations of abolitionists, including Finney, Mann, Emerson, and Olmsted, agreed.

    3. The meaning of racial equality continued to develop, as the later work of Booker T. Washington and Jesse Jackson bore witness.

C. Immigrants and members of later-arriving minorities took seriously the American promise of equality and democracy and tried to realize it in practice.

    1. The examples of such Jewish immigrants as Abraham Cahan and such Hispanics as Roberto Clemente demonstrate this tendency.

    2. In the United States, equality has usually meant equal but different, because diversity is also a highly prized American value.

    3. Equality is also generally identified with equality of opportunity, but with the implication of inequality of outcome; the United States has always opposed coercive government schemes to ensure equality of outcome.

D. A major theme of American history is its political stability.

    1. The United States fosters a system of government in which rival interests can compete but must settle differences peaceably, thus preserving political stability and facilitating economic growth.

    2. At first a revolutionary beacon to the rest of the world, America, by 1917, had become the world leader in antirevolutionary inspiration, opposing communism— eventually, worldwide.

    3. American conservatism is paradoxical, because it entails the attempt to conserve a system created by revolution and characterized by a high degree of dynamism.

E. The American tradition of democracy and equality even has a literary dimension: In his book *Representative Men*, Emerson expounds the idea that truly great men are those who serve their fellow men.

II. Faith in progress, material and moral, coupled with a rejection of fatalism, seem to be among the most basic of all American attributes, and each has a dynamic history of its own.

    A. Explorers determined from the beginning that the United States would grow, enrich itself, and spread its principles as widely as possible.

        1. Lewis and Clark shared with earlier explorers, such as John Smith, a high faith in the American land itself and passed on to such later ones as John Wesley Powell the idea of a continental empire.

        2. Twentieth-century pioneers, such as Charles Lindbergh, linked traditional American virtues with faith in high technology.

        3. The idea of conquering new frontiers is embedded in American lore.

    B. Entrepreneurs created the machines and the goods that underpinned America's development as the wealthiest nation in the history of the world.

        1. Eli Whitney, Andrew Carnegie, and Henry Ford operated brilliantly in the capitalist environment.

        2. The United States has always been a land of opportunity, where individuals could undertake initiatives of their own; private economy has buoyed economic growth.

        3. The expansionist imperative was sometimes heavy-handed, as the work of William Mulholland demonstrates.

    C. Rachel Carson's bestseller, *Silent Spring* (1962) drew attention to environmental problems. The American answer is to improve technology, as opposed to doing away with it, and improve legislation to ensure cleaner industrial processes.

III. The perfectionist impulse made Americans eager to live up to their ideals.

    A. Early American idealists sometimes implied that America was the negation of Europe.

1. More often, though, they sought European approval (as the career of Emerson suggests) and aimed to outstrip the Europeans.
2. By the 20th century, America had become a source of salvation to an endangered Europe, as Herbert Hoover's humanitarian work demonstrated in the era of World War I.
3. By the end of the 20th century, that presented a problem to American foreign policy-makers.

B. An unresolved battle between the forces of Puritanism and emotional expressiveness remains unresolved in the American psyche.
1. Cotton Mather and such heirs as Charles Finney and Horace Mann represent a Puritan tradition that has always been deeply attractive to Americans.
2. A vivid succession of entertainers, including Buffalo Bill, Houdini, Duke Ellington, and Shirley Temple, represent the antithesis of Puritanism.

IV. The reality of American life today falls short of the nation's ideals. But the nation does well by comparison with the actual alternatives in the rest of the world.

Questions to Consider:

1. How does the biographical approach to historical study illuminate themes that might not otherwise become clear?

2. How do current challenges facing the United States affect the national identity, and what resources can the nation draw from as it seeks to meet them?

The American Identity

Practicality

War	Politics
John Smith	William Penn
Frances Marion	Benjamin Franklin
Edmund Ruffin	Thomas Jefferson
William T. Sherman	Abigail Adams
Douglas MacArthur	Oliver W. Holmes
	Samuel Gompers
	William Mulholland
	Booker T. Washington
	Emma Goldman
	Herbert Hoover
	George Wallace
	Shirley Temple
	Jesse Jackson

Pioneers

Inventors and Entrepreneurs
- Benjamin Franklin
- Eli Whitney
- William Cody
- William Mullholland
- Henry Ford
- Al Capone
- Andrew Carnegie
- Rittenhouse and Bartram
- Helen Keller

Explorers
- Lewis and Clark
- John Wesley Powell
- Charles Lindbergh
- John Smith

Artists
- Frederick Olmstead
- Louisa M. Alcott
- Isabella Stewart Gardner
- Abraham Cahan
- Harry Houdini
- Duke Ellington
- Leonard Bernstein
- Shirley Temple
- Roberto Clemente

Idealism

Intellectuals	Humanitarians	Religious Figures
Cotton Mather	Frederick Douglass	William Penn
Benjamin Franklin	Andrew Carnegie	Cotton Mather
Thomas Jefferson	Samuel Gompers	Mother Ann Lee
Edmund Ruffin	Booker T. Washington	Charles G. Finney
Horace Mann	Herbert Hoover	Brigham Young
Ralph Waldo Emerson		Black Elk
John W. Powell		Jesse Jackson
O.W. Holmes		
Emma Goldman		
Betty Friedan		
William F. Buckley		

Timeline

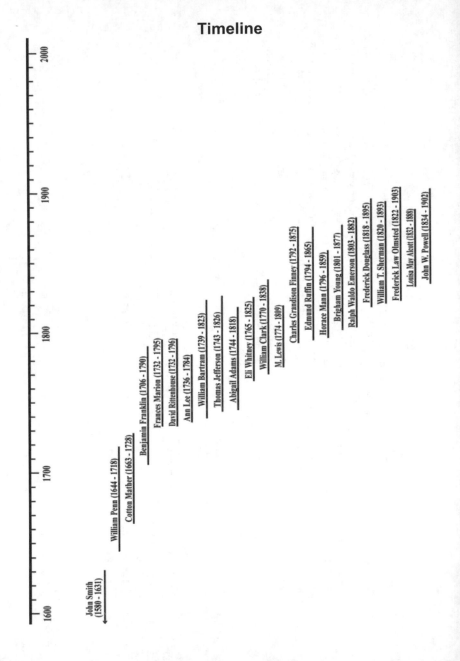

©2005 The Teaching Company.

Andrew Carnegie (1835 - 1919)

Isabella S. Gardner (1840 - 1923)

Oliver W. Holmes (1841 - 1935)

"Buffalo Bill" Cody (1846 - 1917)

Samuel Gompers (1850 - 1924)

William Mulholland (1855 - 1935)

Booker T. Washington (1856 - 1915)

Abraham Cahan (1860 - 1951)

Henry Ford (1863 - 1947)

Black Elk (1863 - 1950)

Emma Goldman (1869 - 1940)

Harry Houdini (1874 - 1926)

Herbert Hoover (1874 - 1964)

Helen Keller (1880 - 1968)

Douglas MacArthur (1880 - 1964)

Al Capone (1899 - 1947)

Duke Ellington (1899 - 1974)

Charles Lindbergh (1902 - 1974)

Leonard Bernstein (1918 - 1990)

George Wallace (1919 - 1998)

Betty Friedan (b. 1921)

William F. Buckley Jr. (b. 1925)

Shirley Temple (b. 1928)

Roberto Clemente (1934 - 1972)

Jesse Jackson (b. 1941)

Glossary

abolitionist: Any American before the Civil War who believed that slavery should be abolished. Some, such as John Brown and Frederick Douglass, were "immediate abolitionists," who favored immediate elimination of slavery, whatever the cost. Others—more socially respectable in their day— were "gradual abolitionists," who feared the social and political upheavals of immediate abolition.

anarchism: The belief, illustrated here in the biographical sketch of Emma Goldman, that all forms of government are corrupt, degrade humanity, and should be eliminated. In its way highly idealistic, anarchism has always been vulnerable to accusations of impracticality. Most Americans of the late 19th and early 20th centuries feared and hated anarchists as bomb-throwing radicals.

antebellum: Before the American Civil War. The term is usually used for the period 1820–1861, whereas *post-bellum* is used for the era 1865–1890.

capitalism: The dominant American economic system, according to which individual entrepreneurs take the risk of establishing businesses in the hope that they can succeed in selling their products, despite the efforts of rivals and competitors. The degree to which capitalism should be regulated by government (to protect workers and consumers) has been a source of constant national controversy.

Cold War: The long standoff between the United States and its allies on one side and the Soviet Union and its satellites on the other side of the "Iron Curtain," between 1945 and 1989.

demagogue: An unscrupulous politician who appeals to, and manipulates, popular prejudices in pursuit of his own political aggrandizement. Well-known American examples include Senator Joseph McCarthy and Alabama governor George Wallace.

democracy: A political system that derives its legitimacy from the consent of majorities, expressed through their votes. More broadly, a society in which the opinions and attitudes of all the inhabitants must be taken into consideration, not just those of the ruling elite.

egalitarianism: Dedication to human equality and striving to achieve equality in a society of apparent inequalities.

equality: In American history, equality as an ideal has usually signified equal opportunities (and unequal outcomes) in the "race" of life, rather than actual material equality. Because advantages are usually passed on from one generation to another, equality has been, throughout American history, a controversial aspiration.

fatalism: The belief or attitude that events cannot be influenced by human action or intervention. Fatalism is notably absent from the ideas and values of the leading Americans studied in this course.

feminism: The belief that invidious discrimination against women is wrong and that the accident of gender should make no difference in an individual's opportunities, except when it is biologically inescapable.

idealism: Aspiring to live up to noble principles and the belief that such an aspiration is right, even when the ideals appear impractical. As a philosophical position, idealism implies the priority of thoughts over material realities, but in the context of this course, the term is used in the first and more common sense.

irrigation: Channeling scarce water resources to crops in areas where rainfall alone is too low for ordinary farming. Irrigation was essential to farming (and to urban development) in the western third of the United States, nearly everywhere west of the 100th meridian of longitude.

meritocracy: A system that depends on the best qualified (most meritorious) people taking leadership positions, as opposed to a system in which wealth or personal connections lead to preferment.

militarism: Domination of a society by its military forces. America's exceptional freedom from militarism, despite its military power, is illustrated in President Truman's dismissal of General MacArthur from his Korean War command when he intervened in the political debate about the war.

pacifism: The belief that war is always wrong. An honorable tradition among a minority of Americans, especially Quakers, beginning with the colonial founder William Penn but recurring in such later non-Quaker figures as the industrialist Henry Ford.

philanthropy: The giving of personal wealth to socially worthwhile causes, such as charities and education, without the expectation of an immediate material return.

pragmatism: The assumption and expectation that a practical solution can be found to most problems, moral, political, and technical, and that ideas are most valuable not in themselves but when converted to some practical use.

religiosity: A term that American conditions have necessitated, indicating a high degree of religious observance but in a wide variety of forms and groupings, most of which are excluded from public life.

socialism: The belief, never widely shared among Americans, that the goods produced by the whole nation should be shared equally by all its citizens and that a benign government should ensure actual equality of distribution.

Bibliography

General Works

Boorstin, Daniel. *The Americans.* 3 vols. New York: Random House, 1958, 1965, 1973. One volume each on America's colonial, national, and democratic experiences, all emphasizing the centrality of American pragmatism and inventiveness.

Franklin, Benjamin. *Autobiography.* New York: Dover, 1996. A good specialized work, but by now, it's a good general work, too, because it has become a byword for American enterprise, industry, and optimism.

Hofstadter, Richard. *The American Political Tradition and the Men Who Made It.* New York: Vintage, 1989 (1948). The most accomplished historian of the post-World War II era explains the nature of American politics—a classic.

Johnson, Paul. *A History of the American People.* New York: Perennial, 1999. Abrasive, opinionated British neoconservative views the Americans, sometimes with sharp insights, at other times with bizarre but always stimulating judgments.

McPherson, James M. *Battle Cry of Freedom: The Civil War Era.* New York: Oxford University Press, 1988. The best one-volume history of the great trauma, which will help you put in context the many Americans mentioned in the course who lived through it.

Phillips, Kevin. *The Cousins Wars: Religion, Politics and the Triumph of Anglo-America.* New York: Basic, 1999. How English influences have played a decisive role in the development of the American character, and the long vitality of Anglo-American relationships.

Potter, David. *People of Plenty: Economic Abundance and the American Character.* Chicago: University of Chicago Press, 1958. Wealth matters most in making America what it is, according to this mid-century classic.

Tocqueville, Alexis de. *Democracy in America.* 2 vols. New York: Vintage, 1990 (1835, 1840). Still the place to begin for any serious study of American identity.

Specialized Works

Akers, Charles W. *Abigail Adams: An American Woman.* Boston: Little Brown, 1980. Good biography of a starchy but somehow likeable Puritan lady with very firm principles.

Alcott, Louisa May. *Little Women*. New York: Grammercy, 1998 (1869). This sentimental novel is also a wonderful historical source on mid-nineteenth century family life in New England

Allitt, Patrick. *Catholic Intellectuals and Conservative Politics in America, 1950–1985*. Ithaca, NY: Cornell University Press, 1993. The author's first venture into print.

Allmendinger, David F., Jr. *Ruffin: Family and Reform in the Old South*. New York: Oxford University Press, 1990. Slaveowner, soldier, and agricultural chemist. This biography sets him in the context of the extended family of which he was patriarch.

Ambrose, Stephen. *Undaunted Courage: Meriwether Lewis, Thomas Jefferson, and the Opening of the American West*. New York: Simon and Schuster/Touchstone, 1996. Best of the dozens of recent books about the plucky duo and excellent on Clark, despite its title.

Andrews, Edward Deming. *The People Called Shakers*. New York: Dover, 1963. Rich account of the sect Mother Ann Lee founded.

Arrington, Leonard. *Brigham Young: American Moses*. New York: Knopf, 1985. Official Mormon historian's book on the venerated leader but not lacking in critical perspective.

Bailey, Anne J. *War and Ruin: William T. Sherman and the Savannah Campaign*. Philadelphia: Scholarly Resources, 2002. Detailed elaboration of Sherman's famous remark "War is Hell."

Bailyn, Bernard. *To Begin the World Anew: The Genius and Ambiguities of the American Founders*. New York: Knopf, 2003. A reminder from a master historians that, for all their faults, the Founders were an astonishingly talented group.

Bak, Richard. *Henry and Edsel: The Creation of the Ford Empire*. New York: John Wiley, 2003. Unvarnished account of the industrial giant and his family in all their strengths and weaknesses.

Barbour, Philip L. *The Three Worlds of Captain John Smith*. Boston: Houghton Mifflin, 1964. Vivid account of the Virginia founder and his many varied adventures.

Bartram, William. *Travels and Other Writings*. Thomas Slaughter, ed. New York: Library of America, 1996. The best way to learn about the naturalist is through his own words—no book about him so far has been remotely as good.

Bergh, A. Scott. *Lindbergh*. New York: Berkeley Publishing Group, 1999. The many facets of Lindbergh's life. Absolves him of allegations of pro-Nazism but shows that he was politically naïve.

Bergreen, Lawrence. *Capone: The Man and the Era*. New York: Simon and Schuster, 1994. There are dozens of dreadful books about Al Capone (the authors yearn to be criminals, apparently) and a few fair ones—do what you can with this imperfect one.

Bernstein, Leonard. *The Unanswered Question: Six Talks at Harvard*. Cambridge, MA: Harvard University Press, 1976. The pianist, conductor and composer theorizing about why music is so pleasurable.

Bernstein, R. B. *Thomas Jefferson*. New York: Oxford University Press, 2003. One of the most readable of the hundreds of biographies.

Beveridge, Charles E., and Paul Rocheleau. *Frederick Law Olmsted: Designing the American Landscape*. New York: Rizzoli, 1995. Sweeping account of the landscape architect and his mark on vast areas throughout the USA.

Brando, Ruth. *The Life and Many Deaths of Harry Houdini*. London: Secker and Warburg, 1993. It's hard to write objectively about a magician and escape-artist, but Brando does what she can to separate the truths from the myths and make it all cohere.

Bringhurst, Newell. *Brigham Young and the Expanding American Frontier*. Boston: Little Brown, 1986. Places the Mormon trek to Utah in the context of the 1840s migrations to Oregon and California.

Bryan, Ford R. *Beyond the Model T: The Other Ventures of Henry Ford*. Detroit: Wayne State University Press, 1990.

———. *Friends, Families, and Forays: Scenes from the Life and Times of Henry Ford*. Detroit: Wayne State University Press, 2002.

Buckley, William F., Jr. *The Unmaking of a Mayor*. New York: Viking, 1966. Hootingly funny account by a candidate who knew he was going to lose the election and therefore could speak truthfully to the major party candidates.

Burner, David. *Herbert Hoover, a Public Life*. New York: Knopf, 1979. Not a page-turner but a valuable book, restoring the much-traduced Hoover to a position of honor in American history.

Burton, Humphrey. *Leonard Bernstein*. New York: Doubleday, 1994.

Butterfield, L. H., et al., eds. *The Book of Abigail and John: Selected Letters of the Adams Family*. Cambridge, MA: Harvard University Press, 1975. He's the really brilliant one but she's never shabby or second rate.

Cabot, James Elliot. *A Memoir of Ralph Waldo Emerson*. Boston: Houghton Mifflin, 1887. The transcendentalist by one of his lifelong friends.

Cahan, Abraham. *The Rise of David Levinsky*. New York: Harper Colophon, 1960 (1917). One of the ten best novels in American history, and one of the best two about the immigrant experience.

Carnegie, Andrew. *Autobiography*. Boston: Northeastern University Press, 1985. Emulate Carnegie's style and you'll never sound unsure of yourself again.

Carter, Dan T. *The Politics of Rage: George Wallace, the Origins of the New Conservatism, and the Transformation of American Politics*. 2nd ed. Baton Rouge, LA: Louisiana State University Press, 2000. Splendid political biography, balanced and steadily insightful about Wallace's wider significance.

Carter, Morris. *Isabella Stewart Gardner and Fenway Court*. Boston: Houghton Mifflin, 1925. How the imperious old lady got her own way about everything.

Carter, Robert A. *Buffalo Bill Cody: The Man behind the Legend*. New York: John Wiley, 2000. Just as it says; what really went on, rather than the folklore and legends.

Cashin, Edward. *William Bartram and the American Revolution on the Southern Frontier*. Columbia, SC: University of South Carolina, 2000. Good on the vast scale and underpopulation of the Carolina lowcountry, and its biological richness.

Chesebrough, David B. *Frederick Douglass: Oratory from Slavery*. Westport, CT: Greenwood, 1998. Helpful guide to the varieties of anti-slavery opinion in the antebellum North.

Davis, Margaret Leslie. *Rivers in the Desert: William Mulholland and the Inventing of Los Angeles*. New York: Harper Collins, 1993. Gripping account of the engineer's audacity and brilliance, as well as his fatal shortcomings.

Dorman, Michael. *The George Wallace Myth*. New York: Bantam, 1976. A vintage specimen in the political debunking tradition.

Douglass, Frederick. *The Narrative of the Life of Frederick Douglass.* New Haven, CT: Yale University Press, 2001 (1845). No book about the abolitionist delivers with as much impact as the ex-slave's own words.

Downs, Robert Bingham. *Horace Mann: Champion of the Public Schools.* New York: Twayne, 1974. There are no exciting books about Mann despite the importance of his work. This one is serviceable but that's about the highest praise you can give it.

Duberman, Martin. *Mother Earth: An Epic Drama of Emma Goldman's Life.* New York: St. Martin's Press, 1991. Even a century after the fact she can infatuate men, and Duberman seems glad to be under the spell.

Dupuis, Richard, and Garth Rosell, eds. *The Memoirs of Charles G. Finney.* Grand Rapids, MI: Academic Books, 1989. Evangelical preaching as high adventure, told by the utterly straightforward and dedicated minister.

Ellis, Joseph. *The American Sphinx: The Character of Thomas Jefferson.* New York: Vintage, 1997. Shrewd and psychologically insightful study of the great one.

Emerson, Ralph Waldo. *The Spiritual Emerson: Essential Writings.* David Robinson, ed. Boston: Beacon Press, 2003.

Falk, Candace. *Love, Anarchy, and Emma Goldman.* New York: Holt, Reinhart, and Winston, 1984. Weep, howl with rage, burn with love, and in other ways, share Goldman's tumultuous emotional life through this sympathetic and entertaining biography.

Fausold, Martin L. *The Presidency of Herbert Hoover.* Lawrence, KS: University Press of Kansas, 1985. Lumbering but informative—not for late at night reading.

Fein, Albert. *Frederick Law Olmsted and the American Environmental Tradition.* New York: George Braziller, 1972. Sets the landscape architect in the wider history of environmental protection and conservation.

Foner, Philip S. *Frederick Douglass.* New York: Citadel, 1964. Former American Communist's insightful biography of the ex-slave and abolitionist spokesman.

Francis, Richard. *Ann the Word: The Story of Ann Lee.* London: Fourth Estate, 2000. The fact of her illiteracy and the fact of her being a religious founder have combined to make Ann Lee a difficult person about whom to write well. This book doesn't solve all the conceptual problems.

Freeberg, Ernest. *The Education of Laura Bridgman*. Cambridge, MA: Harvard University Press, 2001. Brilliant history of Helen Keller's most famous predecessor.

Friedan, Betty. *The Feminine Mystique*. New York: Harper and Row, 2001 (1963). The spark that lit the feminist fire.

Geiter, Mary. *William Penn*. London: Longman, 2000. One of the best among dozens of biographies of the founder—some of which are too reverent to be believed.

Gibbons, Arnold. *Race, Politics and the White Media: The Jesse Jackson Campaigns*. Lanham, MD: University Press of America, 1993. Dry political science style, but full of sensible information about Jackson's political dilemma.

Goldfarb, Hillard T. *The Isabella Stewart Gardner Museum*. New Haven, CT: Yale University Press, 1995. Part guidebook, part history of the lady and her museum.

Goldman, Emma. *Living My Life*. 2 vols. New York: Dover, 1970 (1931). One of the very greatest American autobiographies, by the anarchist.

Gompers, Samuel. *Seventy Years of Life and Labor*. Nick Salvatore, ed. Ithaca, NY: New York State School of Industrial and Labor Relations at Cornell Press, 1984 (1925). AFL founder's autobiography—to be skimmed rather than read unless you want every detail about every meeting he attended.

Gordon, John W. *South Carolina and the American Revolution: A Battlefield History*. Columbia, SC: University of South Carolina, 2003. Useful context for understanding Francis Marion's soldiering career.

Green, Constance. *Eli Whitney and the Birth of American Technology*. Boston: Little Brown, 1956. A reverent biography from a less skeptical age than our own; it accepts most of Whitney's version of events, which many other biographers have challenged.

Greene, Julie. *Pure and Simple Politics: The American Federation of Labor and Political Activism*. Cambridge: Cambridge University Press, 1998. Why Samuel Gompers was so moderate, and why he kept electoral politics at arm's length.

Hadley, Rollin Van, ed. *The Letters of Isabella Stewart Gardner and Bernard Berenson*. Boston: Northeastern University Press, 1987. Generous patron (Gardner) and upstart protégé (Berenson) who was almost too precocious for his own good.

Hammontree, Patsy Guy. *Shirley Temple Black: A Bio-Bibliography*. Westport, CT: Greenwood, 1998.

Hanno, Arnold. *Roberto Clemente: Batting King*. New York: Putnam, 1973. As with most sports biographies, he gets the hagiographical treatment and is made to seem more important than he really was.

Hardesty, Von. *Lindbergh: Flight's Enigmatic Hero*. New York: Harcourt, 2002. Fair-minded exploration of the paradoxes and puzzles of the aviator's life; more necessary than ever in light of Philip Roth's accusation (in *The Plot Against America*) that Lindbergh was a fascist sympathizer.

Hardman, Keith J. *Charles Grandison Finney: Revivalist and Reformer*. Syracuse, NY: Syracuse University Press, 1987. Exhaustive biography of the evangelist for any reader with plenty of leisure.

Harlan, Louis. *Booker T. Washington: The Wizard of Tuskegee*. New York: Oxford University Press, 1986. "Wizard" is just the right word, demonstrating before you have even opened the book that Harlan is the right guide to the race leader's life. But read Washington's *Up from Slavery*, too, if you can.

Hennessee, Judith. *Betty Friedan: Her Life*. New York: Random House, 1999. No screaming fit, jealous rage, or infidelity goes un-analyzed.

Herrmann, Dorothy. *Helen Keller: A Life*. New York: Knopf, 1998. Hard not to get carried away with admiration for the subject, and this book is a good companion to Keller's own *Story of My Life*, which you must not fail to read.

Hindle, Brooke. *David Rittenhouse*. Princeton, NJ: Princeton University Press, 1964. A matter-of-fact biography of the astronomer, demonstrating his eminence to his contemporaries.

Hirshon, Stanley. *The White Tecumseh: A Biography of General William T. Sherman*. New York: John Wiley, 1997. Even-handed biography of a man who still makes pulses race pro- and con-.

Horowitz, Daniel. *Betty Friedan and the Making of the Feminine Mystique: The American Left, the Cold War, and Modern Feminism*. Boston: University of Massachusetts Press, 2000. A merciless but marvelous account of the feminist's complex life and previously obscured political connections.

Horry, Peter, and Parson M. L. Weems. *The Life of General Francis Marion, a Celebrated Partisan Officer in the Revolutionary War*. Philadelphia: Lippincott, 1856 (1824). Weems, the man who invented the story about Washington and the cherry tree from whole cloth now turns the Carolina soldier into a mythical figure

Hounshell, David. *From the American System to Mass Production.* Baltimore: Johns Hopkins University Press, 1984. There are more detailed books about Eli Whitney, but this one is the best at putting Whitney's life and work into the context of American industrial history.

Howe, Irving. *World of Our Fathers: The Journey of the East European Jews to America and the Life They Found and Made.* New York: Simon and Schuster, 1976. Other books will tell you more about the details of Abraham Cahan's life (check Howe's own bibliography), but this is the one you want—definitive on New York Jewish life in the Cahan era.

Howe, Mark de Wolfe. *Justice Oliver Wendell Holmes.* 2 vols. Cambridge, MA: Harvard University Press, 1957, 1963.

Hundley, Norris. *The Great Thirst: Californians and Water.* Berkeley, CA: University of California Press, 1992. Good reminder of a simple truth—there's not much water in California, which makes hydraulic engineers like Mulholland vital historical figures.

Isaacson, Walter. *Benjamin Franklin, an American Life.* New York: Simon and Schuster, 2003. Scintillating—the author is worthy of his subject.

Jones, Landon Y., ed. *The Essential Lewis and Clark.* New York: Harper Collins/Ecco, 2000.

Judis, John. *William F. Buckley, Jr.: Patron Saint of the Conservatives.* New York: Simon and Schuster, 1988. Less fun to read than Buckley's own books, especially *The Unmaking of a Mayor*, and marred by the author's assumption that conservatism is bad and that you'll agree it's bad. Despite these flaws, Judis tells you what's what.

Kasson, John. *Houdini, Tarzan, and the Perfect Man: The White Male Body and the Challenge of Modernity in America.* New York: Hill and Wang, 2001. Sensible ideas dressed up in postmodern jargon.

Kasson, Joy S. *Buffalo Bill's Wild West: Celebrity, Memory and Popular History.* New York: Hill and Wang, 2000.

Kaufman, Stuart B. *Samuel Gompers and the Origins of the American Federation of Labor.* Westport, CT: Greenwood Press, 1973.

Keller, Helen. *The Story of My Life.* New York: Dell, 1961 (1903). The fact that it exists at all is miraculous. The fact that it's a good book by any standards enhances the miracle.

Kelley, Joseph J., Jr. *Pennsylvania: The Colonial Years*. Garden City, NY: Doubleday, 1980. Penn in context—his weaknesses, as well as his strengths, amplified.

Kellock, Harold. *Houdini: The Life Story*. New York: Blue Ribbon, 1928.

Keyser, Elizabeth. *Whispers in the Dark: The Fiction of Louisa May Alcott*. Knoxville, TN: University of Tennessee Press, 1993. The subterranean history of *Little Women* and its creator.

Kirk, John T. *The Shaker World: Art, Life, Belief*. New York: Harry N. Abrams, 1997. Lavish pictorial account of the Shakers' material culture.

Krass, Peter. *Carnegie*. New York: John Wiley, 2002. Does a better job than most Carnegie books by reminding you that there was nothing inevitable about his rise to fame and fortune. Readable, too.

Lash, Joseph P. *Helen and Teacher*. Reading, MA: Addison-Wesley, 1980. More on Helen Keller and her stormy relationship with her teacher.

Lavender, David. *The Way to the Western Sea: Lewis and Clark across the Continent*. New York: Harper and Row, 1988.

Lawlor, Laurie. *Helen Keller: Rebellious Spirit*. New York: Holiday House, 2001.

Lawrence, A. H. *Duke Ellington and His World: A Biography*. New York: Routledge, 2001. Less annoying than most jazz books and full of surprises about the pianist's life.

Lemay, J. A. Leo. *The American Dream of Captain John Smith*. Charlottesville, VA: University Press of Virginia, 1991. More down to earth than you might think from the title, this book puts Smith's American adventures in the context of his other travels and ideas.

Lesher, Stephen. *George Wallace: American Populist*. New York: Perseus, 1994.

Lindbergh, Charles. *The Spirit of St. Louis*. New York: Scribner, 1953. Expanded version of the aviator-hero's first autobiography, written a quarter century after his historic flight.

Livesay, Harold. *Andrew Carnegie and the Rise of Big Business*. New York: Addison-Wesley, 1999. Completely sensible.

———. *Samuel Gompers and Organized Labor in America*. Boston: Little Brown, 1978. A balanced assessment of the AFL leader's life and work, unmarred by the polemics that many labor historians have leveled against him.

MacArthur, Douglas. *Reminiscences*. New York: McGraw Hill, 1964. Completely self-serving.

Manchester, William. *American Caesar: Douglas MacArthur*. Boston: Little Brown, 1978. Manchester's choice of the noun "Caesar" was wickedly appropriate for this compulsively readable but sometimes melodramatic version of the general's life.

Manning, Marable. *Black American Politics: From the Washington Marches to Jesse Jackson*. New York: Schocken, 1985.

Marini, Stephen. *Radical Sects of Revolutionary New England*. Cambridge, MA: Harvard University Press, 1982. A wonderfully well-written reminder that Puritan zeal had not abated by the 1770s and 1780s, at least not in the hills and backcountry of New England.

Markusen, Bruce. *Roberto Clemente: The Great One*. New York: Sports Publishing, 1998.

Marovitz, Stanford E. *Abraham Cahan*. Boston: Twayne, 1996. Like all the Twayne biographies this one has the merit of brevity, clear presentation, and judicious summary.

Mathew, William. *Edmund Ruffin and the Crisis of Slavery in the Old South*. Athens, GA: University of Georgia Press, 1988. Unravels the paradox of the scientist-cum-slave owner.

McCullough, David. *John Adams*. New York: Simon and Schuster, 2001. McCullough is probably the best biographer in America today and has nearly as much to say about Abigail as any of her ostensible biographers. See also his superb works on Theodore Roosevelt and Harry Truman.

McLoughlin, William G. *Charles Grandison Finney to Billy Graham*. New York: Ronald Press, 1959. Where Finney fits in the long history of evangelical revivalists.

McPherson, James M. *Battle Cry of Freedom: The Civil War Era*. New York: Oxford University Press, 1988. Still the best one-volume history of the Civil War, and its documentation will lead you on to the next-best five hundred books.

Mercer, Charles E. *Roberto Clemente*. New York: Putnam, 1974. Most baseball books are star-struck drivel or falsely portentous blither. This one's just a shade better on both counts.

Messerli, Jonathan. *Horace Mann: A Biography*. New York: Knopf, 1972. No thrills here, but a workmanlike account of the educational reformer's achievements.

Middlekauff, Robert. *The Mathers: Three Generations of Puritan Intellectuals*. Berkeley, CA: University of California Press, 1971. Humane, intelligent account of Cotton Mather and his family.

Miller, Douglas T. *Frederick Douglass and the Fight for Freedom*. New York: Facts on File, 1988. Too enthusiastic ever to find fault with its own hero, but informative just the same.

Miller, Perry. *The New England Mind: From Colony to Province*. Cambridge, MA: Belknap of Harvard University Press, 1953. Excellent on Cotton Mather. Miller is the historian who rescued the Puritans' reputation from caricature in the 1930–1950 era.

————, ed. *The Transcendentalists: An Anthology*. Cambridge, MA: Harvard University Press, 1950. Miller's luminously clear and engaging account gives excellent support to the lectures on Emerson and Alcott.

Mitchell, Betty L. *Edmund Ruffin: A Biography*. Bloomington, IN: Indiana University Press, 1981.

Moore, Jacqueline M. *Booker T. Washington, W. E. B. DuBois and the Struggle for Racial Uplift*. Atlanta: Scholarly Resources, 2003. Pious but purposeful, and sets Washington nicely against his most impressive rival.

Morgan, Edmund. *Benjamin Franklin*. New Haven, CT: Yale University Press, 2002. Best single-volume biography of the polymath by one of the premier U.S. historians of our era.

Morris, Nancy. *Puerto Rico*. New York: Praeger, 1995. Colorful background book to go with the lecture on Roberto Clemente.

Morton, Marian. *Emma Goldman and the American Left: Nowhere at Home*. New York: Twayne, 1992.

Mulholland, Catherine. *William Mulholland and the Rise of Los Angeles*. Berkeley, CA: University of California Press, 2000. A descendant's unsuccessful attempt to vindicate the careless engineer's reputation.

Murray, George. *The Legacy of Al Capone: Portraits and Annals of Chicago's Public Enemies*. New York: Putnam, 1975.

Myers, Paul. *Leonard Bernstein*. London: Phaidon, 1998. In this controversial book Myers "outed" Bernstein by describing his homosexuality in detail.

Nash, George. *The Conservative Intellectual Movement in America Since 1945*. New York: Basic, 1979. Best account so far of the recent nation-changing conservative movement and how it got started.

————. *The Life of Herbert Hoover*. 3 vols. New York: Norton, 1983. This is by far the fullest and best account, but these volumes take the story only as far as the Treaty of Versailles.

Nash, Lee, ed. *Understanding Herbert Hoover: Ten Perspectives*. Stanford, CA: Hoover Institution Press, 1987.

Neihardt, John. *Black Elk Speaks*. Lincoln, NE: University of Nebraska Press, 1979 (1932). Generations of readers have let the rhetoric sweep them away as they sink into the mystical world of the Sioux holy man.

Nelson, Lee, ed. *A Prophet's Journal: Brigham Young's Own Story in His Own Words*. Provo, UT: Council Press, 1980. He wasn't very well educated and it shows.

Nevins, Allan, and Frank Hill. *Ford: The Times, the Man, the Company*. New York: Scribner's, 1954. Old but good biography of the automaker by an excellent and stylish writer.

Nicholson, Stuart. *Reminiscing in Tempo: A Portrait of Duke Ellington*. Boston: Northeastern University Press, 1999.

Noble, David. *Forces of Production: A Social History of Industrial Automation*. New York: Knopf, 1984. How the machines became more lifelike and the poor workers became more robotic.

Novick, Sheldon. *Honorable Justice: the Life of Oliver Wendell Holmes*. New York: Laurel, 1989. Devote a hundred hours to this hefty biography and you'll be a Holmes expert. Or browse it selectively for the best parts and skip lightly over the others.

Oakes, James. *The Ruling Race: A History of American Slaveholders*. New York: Knopf, 1982. Excellent and never self-righteous or superior—he manages to show their complexity.

Ostling, Richard, and Joan Ostling. *Mormon America: The Power and the Promise*. New York: Harper Collins, 1999. This general history of the Mormons will give you a wider perspective on Brigham Young and his successors than Arrington's biography.

Peare, Catherine Owens. *William Penn: A Biography*. Philadelphia: Lippincott, 1957.

Perrett, Geoffrey. *Old Soldiers Never Die: The Life of Douglas MacArthur*. New York: Random House, 1996. Perrett is a first-rate historian of the World War II era, and here, he replaces the heat of MacArthur controversy, of which there has been much, with bright, clear light.

Peterson, Merrill. *Thomas Jefferson and the New Nation.* New York: Oxford University Press, 1970. Huge but readable story of his life, one of literally hundreds of Jefferson biographies.

Pisano, Dominick. *Charles Lindbergh and the Spirit of St. Louis.* Washington, DC: Smithsonian National Air and Space Museum, 2002.

Posner, Richard A., ed. *The Essential Holmes: Selections from the Letters, Speeches, Judicial Opinions and Other Writings of Oliver Wendell Holmes.* Chicago: University of Chicago Press, 1996. Holmes lived for so long and was involved in so many activities, it's hard to make an anthology like this coherent.

Powell, John Wesley. *The Exploration of the Colorado River and Its Canyons.* New York: Penguin, 1987 (1875). Magnificent description of the desperate first descent, in unpowered wooden boats and the explorers' death-defying feats.

Powers, William K. *Oglala Religion.* Lincoln, NE: University of Nebraska Press, 1977. Deep background for Black Elk.

Rankin, Hugh F. *Francis Marion: The Swamp Fox.* New York: Crowell, 1973. Plodding but serviceable account—relentlessly demythologizes Marion.

Reisner, Marc. *Cadillac Desert: The American West and Its Disappearing Water.* New York: Viking Penguin, 1986. The best general book on western water supplies and how they have been manipulated by such men as Powell and Mulholland.

Rischin, Moses, ed. *Grandma Never Lived in America: The New Journalism of Abraham Cahan.* Bloomington, IN: University of Indiana Press, 1985.

Ronda, James. *Lewis and Clark among the Indians.* Lincoln, NE: University of Nebraska Press, 1984. They were observant, unsentimental, and tried to make sure they kept the upper hand in every encounter, by force if necessary.

Rosenberg, Rosalind. *Divided Lives: American Women in the Twentieth Century.* New York: Hill and Wang, 1992. Where feminism came from and why it struck such a chord after Betty Friedan.

Rusk, Ralph. *The Life of Ralph Waldo Emerson.* New York: Scribner's, 1949. Not great, but steadily informative.

Rybczynski, Witold. *A Clearing in the Distance: Frederick Law Olmsted and America in the Nineteenth Century*. New York: Scribner's, 1999. Superb recent biography of the great park-builder.

Saxton, Martha. *Louisa May: A Modern Biography of Louisa May Alcott*. New York: Avon, 1977. Sizzling feminist take on the novelist's life, packed with good ideas but not always believable.

Schaller, Michael. *Douglas MacArthur: The Far Eastern General*. New York: Oxford University Press, 1996. Underlines the fact that for more than two decades MacArthur never even visited America, even as he became one of its most important men.

Schoenberg, Robert J. *Mr. Capone*. New York: William Morrow, 1992.

Secrest, Meryle. *Leonard Bernstein: A Life*. New York: Knopf, 1994. Almost but not quite a hatchet job; Secrest reveals the secret of Bernstein's homosexual promiscuity but also has a lot of useful insight into his musical achievements.

Shand-Tucci, Douglas. *The Art of Scandal: The Life and Times of Isabella Stewart Gardner*. New York: Harper Collins, 1997. Weird, self-indulgent biography by an intrusive author who really wants to tell you about his own life rather than hers. Sharp and incisive even so.

Sherman, William T. *Memoirs*. Charles Royster, ed. New York: Library of America, 1990. Sherman tells his own story best, but Royster helps us nicely with the more obscure passages.

Shy, John. *A People Numerous and Armed: Reflections on the Military Struggle for American Independence*. New York: Oxford University Press, 1976. Best book on the military history of the American Revolution, especially as it was fought in the South by Francis Marion and others.

Silverman, Kenneth. *The Life and Times of Cotton Mather*. New York: Harper and Row, 1984. A psychoanalytical biography, pushily theoretical in places but ingenious in others.

———, ed. *Selected Letters of Cotton Mather*. Baton Rouge, LA: Louisiana State University Press, 1971.

Slotkin, Richard. *Gunfighter Nation: The Myth of the Frontier in the Twentieth Century*. New York: Atheneum, 1992. Classic on Americans with guns and useful here as a companion to the Buffalo Bill lecture.

Smith, John. *Complete Works*. Philip L. Barbour, ed. Chapel Hill: University of North Carolina Press, 1986. Includes his numerous accounts of Jamestown.

Smith, Merritt Roe. "Eli Whitney and the American System of Manufacturing." In *Technology in America: A History of Individuals and Ideas*, Carroll W. Pursell, ed. Cambridge, MA: MIT Press, 1990.

Stegner, Wallace. *Beyond the Hundredth Meridian: John Wesley Powell and the Second Opening of the West*. Boston: Houghton Mifflin, 1954. As good as a novel and written by a novelist who was also a first-rate western historian.

Stern, Madeleine. *Louisa May Alcott, A Biography*. Boston: Northeastern University Press. 1999. Explains who did what, where, when, and why in the novelist's family.

Stevenson, Elizabeth. *Park-Maker: A Life of Frederick Law Olmsted*. New York: Macmillan, 1977. Central Park beautifies land that used to be a festering slum. Olmsted improved every place he touched.

Temple, Shirley. *Child Star: An Autobiography*. New York: McGraw Hill, 1988. Devoid of the magic that had made her so exquisite as a kiddie.

Timmerman, Kenneth. *Shakedown: Exposing the Real Jesse Jackson*. Chicago: Henry Regnery, 2004. A ruthless assault on the African-American politician but one that scores many palpable hits.

Tucker, Mark, ed. *The Duke Ellington Reader*. New York: Oxford University Press, 1993.

Utley, Robert M. *The Last Days of the Sioux Nation*. New Haven, CT: Yale University Press, 1963. Explanation of why the plains Indians' way of life was bound to come to an end when the whites arrived in significant numbers.

Vaughan, Alden T. *American Genesis: Captain John Smith and the Founding of Virginia*. Boston: Little Brown, 1975. Classic account of Jamestown's early struggles.

Wall, Joseph Frazier. *Andrew Carnegie*. Pittsburgh: University of Pittsburgh Press, 1989.

Washington, Booker T. *Up from Slavery*. New York: Dover, 1995 (1901). You'd have to have a heart of stone not to be impressed by the ex-slave's struggle for self-improvement. Unfortunately, this is a book that gets steadily less interesting as its subject ages and becomes, in effect, a bureaucrat.

White, G. Edward. *Justice Oliver Wendell Holmes: Law and the Inner Self*. New York: Oxford University Press, 1995.

White, John. *Black Leadership in America: From Booker T. Washington to Jesse Jackson*. New York: Addison Wesley, 1990. Nearly all of these leaders were clergymen, but Washington was the exception who proved the rule.

Wildes, Harry E. *William Penn*. New York: Macmillan, 1974.

Wills, Garry. *Inventing America: Jefferson's Declaration of Independence*. New York: Random House, 1978. Brilliantly imaginative and persuasive account of how Jefferson thought, wrote, and lived.

Wilson, R. L. *Buffalo Bill's Wild West: An American Legend*. New York: Random House, 1998. How the show transformed show-business in America and transformed Americans' image of the west itself.

Withey, Lynne. *Dearest Friend: A Life of Abigail Adams*. New York: Free Press, 1981. A puritanical account of a puritanical First Lady.

Worster, Donald. *A River Running West: The Life of John Wesley Powell*. New York: Oxford University Press, 2002. Worster is incapable of writing a dull sentence, and this book is an intellectual feast.

Wright, G. Frederick. *Charles Grandison Finney: American Religious Leader*. New York: Schmul Publishing, 1996. A contemporary evangelical meditates on one of his most important predecessors.

Zierold, Norman. *The Child Stars*. New York: Coward-McCann, 1965. The book you turn to with a sinking heart when you realize that everything by and about Shirley Temple is bad.

Notes

Notes

Notes

Notes

Notes

Notes